PRAISE FOR THE
GOD ALLOWS U-TURNS SERIES

"The bite-sized chapters should be savored one or two at a time, like chocolates from a sampler." Publishers Weekly

"When you need a picker-upper, this is the book to pick up." CBA Marketplace

"If you wonder if you, or your life, can ever change, start reading and discover that Christ is the original Author of *U-Turns for Humans.*" BECKY FREEMAN
National Speaker, Best-Selling Author

"The real-life accounts in this edition of *God Allows U-Turns [A Woman's Journey]* will encourage you to look to the future with renewed confidence." MARY HUNT
Author of *Debt-Proof Living*

"This book *[More God Allows U-Turns]* will inspire you to new hope and greater healing in your relationship with God and those you love." PAUL ESHLEMAN
Director, The JESUS Film Project

"It's good to know that God not only allows U-Turns, he uses them to steer us toward our destiny. What an encouraging word for those going through the fire!" MICHELLE MCKINNEY H...

Author (

D1490571

"The down-to-earth stories speak to the reader in a soft, easy-to-understand depth that penetrates the soul and causes you to want to turn your life in the right direction."　　　Thelma Wells

Women of Faith Speaker, Author

GOD ALLOWS U-TURNS
AMERICAN MOMENTS

TRUE STORIES
OF HOPE AND HEALING
FROM TIMES OF NATIONAL CRISIS

ALLISON GAPPA BOTTKE
with Cheryll Hutchings

PROMISE PRESS
An Imprint of Barbour Publishing

The author is represented by Alive Communications Inc., 7680 Goddard St., Suite 200, Colorado Springs, CO 80920.

Published by Promise Press, an imprint of Barbour Publishing, Inc., P.O. Box 719, Uhrichsville, Ohio 44683, www.promisepress.com.

 Member of the
Evangelical Christian
Publishers Association

Printed in the United States of America.

"The Lord is my light and my salvation—whom shall I fear?
The Lord is the stronghold of my life—of whom shall I be afraid?"
PSALM 27:1

IN HONOR

. . .of all our leaders and personal heroes in times of crisis
who inspire us with their courage, wisdom, and empathy.

IN MEMORY

Betty Lou Thomas
My Minnesota Mom

*"Stampin' up in God's kingdom.
You left an unforgettable imprint on the
hearts and souls of your loved ones."*

CONTENTS

We live in the greatest country of the world—truly the land of the free and the home of the brave. Sometimes we take our country for granted. That's why we must take time to remember American Moments. As we look at what our history, our ancestors, and we have passed through, we realize afresh the things that make America so wonderful.

As we reflect on American Moments, we feel the commitment of those who survived the long voyage from British rule to freedom. . .we feel the thankfulness of those who sat at the table with the Indians at the beginning of a harsh winter. . .we feel the pride of Francis Scott Key in 1814 as, from a ship, he watched our flag rise in triumph after fierce combat with the British.

Focusing on American Moments, we also remember times when we were our own enemy. In 1861 to 1865 when the Civil War brought more deaths than any other war in history. . .when brothers fought brothers as their convictions drove them. . . when we as a nation purged ourselves from the blight of slavery.

As we reflect on American Moments, we reflect that disease and the fury of nature can feel like God's wrath. Small pox, typhus, typhoid fever, yellow fever, and scarlet fever wiped out entire families and communities, and threatened the future of our nation. Americans have also faced natural tragedies with dignity and faith in our Living God. We've been battered, twisted, and drowned by hurricanes, tornadoes, and floods. Through the "Dirty '30s," drought and wind erosion drove thousands of hungry Americans from their homes and farmlands, desperate for food and work. But the American spirit was not destroyed. By

God's grace, we made it through.

As Davenant said, "Faith lights us through the dark to Deity." During the shadowy times, especially, we have turned to God for a reason. . .or answer. . .or direction. For instinctively, in their hearts, Americans have known that only God can provide direction and light.

When the entire world turned upside down, as in the World Wars, Americans looked to their faith as a roadmap.

When our economy became nearly nonexistent, as during the Depression, we drew on, "I have never seen the righteous forsaken or their children begging bread"(Psalm 37:25). Even when we were begging, we believed it would come to an end. . .and it did.

Americans have not only survived, but have learned from each tragedy. In November 1963, while America stood motionless, we learned that a man may be empowered by position, but he is still just a man. In the '60s and '70s, we learned the price is not only high when we fight for our own freedom, but also when we strive to help others retain independence.

After the turbulence of Vietnam, the world of the '80s seemed to calm outwardly. But Americans bounded in confusion as we analyzed our priorities and turned our focus to ourselves—the "Me Generation." However, when we focus on ourselves, we do not see God. Friedrich Nietzsche once said, "God is dead," and during the '80s, many Americans seemed to choose to believe it was true.

It wasn't.

Our focus returned to God through more American Moments. The collaboration of science, man, and nature exploded during the 1986 *Challenger* Disaster, reminding us that the wisdom of man can fail. In the aftermath of the "Me Generation," students denied the sanctity of others' lives, entering schoolhouses with enough arsenal for a war, leaving blood-bathed teenagers in the wake. Adult men began to destroy the living through acts of terror.

And then, near the beginning of the 21st Century, our lives and our trust were shattered on September 11, 2001. About 187 years after Key penned his lasting tribute to "Old Glory," we raised the Stars and Stripes over the rubble. . .we were bruised, but still the land of the free and the home of the brave. America dropped to its knees in shock, and we cried to God with our families. . .with our government. . .with our brothers and sisters. Suddenly we realized the preciousness of life, and of our nation. We forgave each other and the mistakes of the past. We passionately proclaimed: We are the United States of America.

Wind, war, disease, and terrorism may rock Americans, but we will stand firm as a nation built on a faith in a God who accepts every U-Turn we make. Though we are a young nation among the world's power and have been pushed to the end of our tethers, we have overcome. We have endured with faith, struggled with our trust in God, and united through prayer. God Allows U-Turns, and America Moments lets us experience these moments again. Through them we can learn lessons, we can better understand our nation's history, and best of all, we can remember how God delivered and guided us in the past. . .and how He will do so in all of the American Moments of the future.

EVA MARIE EVERSON
Author, Speaker, Teacher

GOD'S PLAN

"I know the plans I have for you," declares the Lord,
". . .plans to give you hope and a future."
JEREMIAH 29:11

GOD REWARDS GOOD DEEDS

by Patricia Laye, Cuthbert, Georgia,
as told by Jim Rogers

f I had not known how to type, I wouldn't be here today," I told my friend. I was returning to Normandy, France, for the first time since 1944. But I wasn't prepared for this surge of overwhelming feelings and memories.

"How did typing save you?" my friend asked.

My mind flew back over the years. During the spring of 1944, at age nineteen, I was drafted and eventually landed in Fort Dix, New Jersey, to be shipped out to England. The invasion of Europe appeared imminent.

One day I was leaving the mess hall when an officer asked, "Can anyone here type?"

Nobody spoke. In boot camp, I'd learned never to volunteer. The major asked again. Suddenly I thought about the men who were already fighting. I figured the least I could do was type. "I typed in high school," I said meekly.

The major glared at me. "What's your name, soldier?"

"Private First Class Jim Rogers, sir."

The major grinned. "Fine. Come along with me, Private Rogers."

For the next few weeks I typed supply orders and kept records. One day the major said, "Private Rogers, your company is shipping out to England. I can't keep you any longer. I have to transfer you back to your company."

He added, "My company will be shipping over soon too. When I get to England, I will request that you work for me again."

Several weeks later I was transferred to the major's staff and worked there until the D-Day Invasion. When the first troops shipped out, he told me, "Well, Private Rogers, looks like this is it. I'm sending you back to your company. Good luck and God be with you."

As I left, the major said, "Private Rogers, you're a special fellow. Lots of men in that mess hall at Fort Dix could type, but you were the only one with the guts to volunteer."

"I felt it was the least I could do to help in this war." This conversation embarrassed me.

"Someday, Private Rogers, that caring will be rewarded. God never forgets when a person helps his fellow man."

Two weeks later I was standing in the middle of Rommel's Panzer Division in France. As we scrambled into landing boats, I remembered the casualties we'd heard of on D-Day. As the boats rode the rough waves, I stared at the cliffs, marveling at how our troops had scaled those steep embankments to take out the German-held concrete bunkers.

The cold spray soaked our clothes, and I tasted the salty ocean. Everyone was nervous. Some prayed silently, others aloud. No other sound rose from my group. After we hit the beach, we marched up the sandy shoal and entered Normandy.

"Toss your duffel bags onto the truck on your right! Climb aboard the truck on your left," a sergeant snapped. "Keep your rifles and ammunition ready. You're in the war now, troops."

Our driver raced down the bombed highway past bullet-riddled houses and through tattered countryside. Suddenly the truck screeched to a halt. "All out!" he shouted. Sympathy crossed his face. "God bless you all!"

I heard firing and knew we were near the front lines.

Our gear never arrived. With only the clothes on our backs and our ammunition, we pushed toward Germany, fighting, marching, resting, moving forward again. My G.I. boots had never fit properly, so my heels blistered, but we marched on. In the following months I developed an infected tendon. With the field medics busy treating life-threatening injuries, I was ashamed to complain. We marched hour upon tiring hour while the pain in my foot and leg grew worse.

I didn't know anything about blood poisoning, and by late November red streaks ran up my throbbing leg. I had a raging fever and was sure I was going to die. Finally, I told my buddies, "I can't march another step. I'm going to die anyway, so I'm stopping."

They didn't want to leave me, but shells fell all around, and they saw I couldn't make it much farther. We wished each other luck. I hobbled to a barn and settled on the hay. I asked God to let me die before the Germans found me. Then I fell asleep.

I don't know how long I slept, but the sound of an approaching vehicle woke me. I wanted to hide but was too weak to move. I closed my eyes and prayed that if the Germans found me, God would let them kill me immediately. The hum of the vehicle grew louder. I waited, my gun propped in my sweaty hands. Suddenly I heard brakes screech. Without opening my eyes I prayed.

"What are you doing here, Private Rogers?" an American voice called.

I explained that I had a serious infection and was waiting to die.

"Help the fellow to the jeep," the officer ordered his driver.

When I reached the jeep, I saw the major I had worked

for in supplies. He shook his head. "You're in a devil of a mess, G.I. You did me a favor once, so I reckon it's time to pay you back."

The major took me to the nearest field hospital. "If you make it, soldier," he said, "let me know. I'll request your transfer to my department. You're the best typist I've had."

With penicillin, the doctors saved my leg. When I recovered, I served on the major's staff for the rest of the war.

"Have you ever seen the major again?" my friend asked.

"No, but I've never refused to do someone a favor since that day. I always remember how God rewarded my good deed in France. Doing the major a favor at Fort Dix is the reason I'm alive."

As we walked back to our tour bus, I thought about Paul's words in 2 Timothy 4:7–8 (KJV): "I have fought a good fight, I have finished my course, I have kept the faith: Henceforth there is laid up for me a crown of righteousness, which the Lord, the righteous judge, shall give me at that day: and not to me only, but unto all them also that love his appearing."

SURVIVOR'S BLOOD

by Maureen Schmidgall,
Libertyville, Illinois

Seventeen-year-old Ross Henry Gilbert itched to see the world, and in 1939, the U.S. Navy was his ticket. As second class boiler tender, Sailor Gilbert's first assignment was aboard the U.S.S. *Oklahoma*, from which he saw only America's west coast. To see more of the world, Ross volunteered to join the Asiatic fleet. He saw Hawaii, Guam, Japan, China, and then the Philippines.

General MacArthur had left the Forty-First Marines and a handful of navy ships to protect Manila and surrounding islands. Ross was on one of those gunboats, the U.S.S. *Luzon.*

One night in December, Ross was on shore leave and returned to a blacked-out bay. He learned Pearl Harbor had just been bombed, and the *Oklahoma* had been capsized by five torpedoes. About 415 men lost their lives on that ship. America was at war.

That war arrived in Manila Bay just as sailors finished their Christmas dinner. From his station in the boiler room, Ross heard the shellfire—it sounded like popcorn exploding. The ship was bombed that night and all the next day. The sailors knew they were outnumbered. The Japanese would soon control the area. Orders came to scuttle the *Luzon* and other ships to keep them out of enemy hands. Hundreds of sailors were left without ships, and Ross ended up at Fort Mills on the tiny island of Hughes. The sailors, trained to fight on ships, not land, were given the higher ground—with a gun that was useless because its pivot arm was missing. They found little food or fresh water—only a few barrels of water, coated with algae.

The soldiers and sailors hung on. Bataan surrendered first, paving the way for the Death March. Corregidor and Fort Drum soon followed, along with Hughes, where Ross fought a land battle beside Filipino and U.S. soldiers. They were under shellfire most of that time. After two months, they had to surrender.

That was the beginning of Ross's three and a half years as a POW. First, he was taken to Clark Field, where the death march began. By now the Japanese had perfected their original Bataan Death March. The prisoners taken from Corregidor, Fort Drum, and Hughes were forced on a parallel march.

After being marched for hours, the soldiers were packed, standing, into boxcars. They had one bucket as a latrine for the few who could get to it. Worse, many men suffered from dysentery. Each prisoner had filled his canteen with water, but the canteens weren't refilled for three days—when they reached the next camp.

These several thousand prisoners proved humans could live on rice balls or "soupy greens" twice a day. Each prisoner was called by a number. Ross was now 7 at one camp and 591 in another. For medicine they received dried blood cubes from the occasional slaughter of an animal. Some guards were cruel, a few were not. But all guards clearly thought it was better to be dead than to be a prisoner of war.

"Doctors" came to camp to inject prisoners for testing. At other times prisoners were taken to undergo unspeakable tests. Ross survived several injections. He was blessed with a strong will to live. It was easy to tell if a prisoner had given up hope; he'd give away his food and be dead in three days.

For three years, Ross was at Manila's Bilibid Prison, and then taken to a disease-ridden camp near Cabanatuan. Then he was sent to a work camp in Mukden, Manchuria. In Manila Bay he saw his old ship, the *Luzon,* which the Japanese had raised and refitted.

In Mukden, Ross worked at a factory that turned metal into machine gun ammunition casings. But Ross and the others often sabotaged machinery. Each day Ross was taken to the gate of the POW camp, searched, marched to the factory, then searched again. Each evening, the procedure was repeated. All along he was called *Gohyaku kyuju ichi,* 591 in Japanese.

Ross started out to see the world, but in prison camp, he only wanted to see home. He just wanted to get married, have children, and live in peace. His prayers and those plans kept him going. Sometimes God's protection sees us through plans we make for ourselves—because He has a plan for our lives too. And He had a plan for Ross.

After the Russians freed Ross, military doctors told him he probably would never have children. He'd been on a near-starvation diet for years and weighed around one hundred pounds. He'd suffered malaria, beriberi, jaundice, malnutrition, and bombing wounds.

That doctor didn't know about God's plan. Ross Henry Gilbert is my father. I'm one of six kids. . .living legacies of how God helps us flourish even when our plans are detoured.

When I asked Dad what got him through prison camp, he said he prayed and read the Bible. God modeled in Sailor Ross Gilbert an example of what it takes to follow through on a U-Turn—God carrying you when you can't carry yourself.

A little more than a year after my oldest son was born, he was diagnosed with Fragile X Syndrome, a genetic form of mental retardation. At that point, I realized God had given us survivor's blood through my father. If he could survive what he did, we could survive too. After all, we have all been given survivor's blood because of what our Lord has done for us.

SAFE AGAIN?

by Sara Houy,
Littleton, Colorado

G et down! There's a guy with a gun! Get under the tables!"

My art teacher ran into the library screaming at us. *What's going on?* I wondered. We'd all heard popping noises that sounded like paintball guns. Probably just a senior prank.

When she realized no one had moved, she yelled louder. "You guys, this is serious! Get down!"

I crawled under the table with my older brother, Seth, and my friend Crystal. We had planned to go out for lunch, but decided to hang out in the library instead. Now, huddling under a table, and unable to see anything else in the library, we wondered what was happening.

The popping noises got louder and sounded bigger than paintball guns. An explosion shook the floor. The cafeteria, always packed at lunch, was directly below us. My brother said, "I don't know what's going on, but I think we'd better pray."

Moments later, we heard blasting outside the library and two gunmen came in. "Everybody stand up!" If Seth's eyes hadn't told me to stay under the table, I probably would have stood.

"We've been waiting to do this our whole lives!" a shooter yelled. "This is for the people who've made fun of us. We're going to kill all the jocks. If you're a jock, you're going to die!"

"We're going to blow up this library!" they shouted, as they fired their guns again and again.

The shooters made their way around the room. They

stopped and asked people questions about their race or religion, and then fired. They taunted their victims before shooting. As the gunmen approached our section, I heard them make a crude comment to a guy about his race. Later I realized it was Isaiah Shoels. Then I heard shots fired. They were loud because only a bookshelf separated our table from Isaiah's. I kept thinking, *This can't be real. Not at my school. Not at Columbine.*

The noise level was deafening, with the gunfire, the bombs, people begging for their lives, and the constant wail of the fire alarm. Suddenly I realized that Seth, Crystal, and I were all praying aloud.

"God," I begged, "please protect us and send your angels. Please give me courage." At that moment God gave me amazing inner peace. Explosions kept going off downstairs and in the library. Tiny pieces of metal and rocks rained on the library table above us. Still, I knew in my heart that God was with us.

The gunmen got to our area. Seth had his arms around Crystal and me. I expected to get shot. I wondered what it would feel like when the bullet entered me.

"God," I prayed, "if I do get shot, please take away the pain."

The shooters came down our aisle and stopped at a table near us.

"Who's under there?" they asked.

A boy answered, and one of them said, "We like you. You can go." I saw his feet run by our table and thought we were next—but the shooters stopped at the table beside ours. They looked under it and saw Daniel Mauser. They called him a name, and I heard more shots.

This is it, I thought.

When they reached our table, one of them pushed in a chair, and it hit me in the head. I didn't budge. Then, for some reason, they just moved on. They had stopped at every other table in our section. Sometimes they said, "You guys are pathetic." Sometimes they shot. But when they came to our table, it was as if they didn't even know we were there. It's a miracle we hadn't been shot.

After a few moments, we heard one say he'd run out of ammo. The other said he'd dropped his clip. Then it got quiet. We could still hear the fire alarm and people moaning, but the gunmen seemed to be gone. Suddenly, people ran by our table to the emergency exit at the back of the library.

"We've got to go now," Seth said, moving toward the door.

I couldn't move. Neither could Crystal. Seth grabbed us both by the arms and pulled us up. I felt like I was dreaming and this was my worst nightmare.

When I stood, I was surprised by the thick smoke from the gunfire and bombs. Blood covered the floor and several tables. As Seth pulled me toward the exit, I saw a boy still crouched under a computer desk, his head covered in blood. I tried to stop, but Seth kept pulling me—he knew it was too late.

As we ran from the building, two cops directed us behind a police car parked near the exit.

The scene behind that car was chaos. Many students were bleeding, with only two officers to help. I heard someone crying for help. I didn't even recognize my friend Kacey at first. She had a softball-sized hole in her shoulder—and it was bleeding profusely. I held a guy's shirt over the wound. I didn't know if it helped, but I had to do something. Then bullets started flying over us again.

The shooters were exchanging gunfire with the cops

hiding with us. *Please, God, watch over us,* I prayed. Finally, another police car pulled up, and more officers began shooting. The gunmen went back into the school.

Before long, police cars started picking us up. They took the wounded first, then people who were hysterical. I was one of the last four taken from the scene.

I later learned that my friend Cassie Bernall was taken from us that day. Cassie was amazing. Although she wasn't perfect, she lived her faith boldly. She was in a different section of the library that day, so we didn't hear the shooters ask if she believed in God. I could have told you she would say yes. She was ready.

God has taught me so much since the tragedy at Columbine. I've wondered why we survived when many others were killed or hurt. I believe God let me survive this horrible experience so He can use me to advance His kingdom. I've been given the opportunity to examine my life and ask what I'd be willing to die for. God changed my life that day. People ask how I've been able to return to school and feel safe again. I don't worry about being safe. My focus from now on is to be ready. Are you?

Previously printed in *Guideposts for Teens,* February/March 2001.

SHOTS ECHOED 'ROUND THE WORLD

by Sandy Austin,
Lakewood, Colorado

S creaming sirens. Hovering helicopters. Flashing lights. Yellow crime tape. No amount of training could ever have prepared me for what I was about to face.

Frightened students streamed out of Columbine with hands on their heads like criminals. Mothers cradled shell-shocked daughters. Fathers ran to embrace their sons. The TV scenes mesmerized us until our assistant principal broke our fixed gaze. "All school district counselors need to report to Columbine immediately. Go!"

I ran to my car and headed toward Columbine. I desperately prayed, "Lord, what do I say to those people? Please give me the right words for each person."

Columbine was blocked off, and I was sent to Leawood Elementary, three blocks away. Cars jammed the roads. Streams of people darted between cars. Media vans jumped the curbs to park on the grass. Police swarmed the area on ground and in the air. My heart was racing. "Help me calm down, Lord. Please help me."

At 1:30 P.M., I squeezed my way through hordes of people and media, flashing my I.D. Chaos reigned inside Leawood's gym. Lines of parents clinging to their kids signed their names to leave the pandemonium.

Confused frenzy enveloped the gym as buses arrived with the precious cargo from Columbine and the students were corralled to the stage at the far end. Parents screamed in joy and relief as they saw their frightened teenagers arrive.

Yet, for other parents, the wait continued.

"God, lead me to the people You want to reach through me," I prayed as I mingled. A couple nearby caught my attention. I eased over to them, introduced myself, and asked whom they were waiting for. The mother responded, "Our son. Justin Thompson. I'm Kim, and this is my husband, Dave." I sensed that they didn't want to talk. I told them I would listen for Justin's name too. "Lord, be with Justin wherever he is, and be with Kim and Dave too," I prayed.

The lists of names from the buses continued to ring out. At times, when I missed hearing the names, I caught the Thompsons' eyes. Each time, they shook their heads. The hours dragged on, fewer buses came, and the gym atmosphere grew more solemn.

At around 6:30 P.M., a deafening silence fell on the crowd as they learned no more buses would arrive from Columbine. I looked at the Thompsons and saw their heads drop. Several people were around them, and I was glad they had friends to support them. About seventeen families still waited for word.

Officials announced that they wouldn't be able to get final word on the students for hours. They said they needed detailed information from parents about their kids, including dental records. Gasps rang out. The officials assured the parents that their sons and daughters could still be hiding, but acknowledged that there were definitely fatalities.

People prayed around the Thompsons and several led Kim home since it would be hours before they could know anything definite. Soon Dave left with another circle of friends.

At 9:30 P.M., I left Leawood exhausted. The exhaustion lasted for days, as I spent long hours counseling students and parents.

Four days after the shootings, I saw a picture in the newspaper of Kim and Dave Thompson at their son's funeral. All the emotions I felt that day at Leawood flooded me. I couldn't get the Thompsons off my mind. For several months, I prayed daily for them. I was guarded about dealing with my own grief. I knew I would counsel in the Columbine area all summer and had to be strong for others. I would have to heal later.

Typically, the hardest time after a tragedy is several months later. The shock wears off, grief is more intense, and the support subsides. Some think the person should be "over it by now" and expect the person to "get on with life."

In the middle of the summer, I wrote a letter to Kim to validate her and her grieving process. A few months later, I saw her at a women's conference luncheon. I was anxious to see how she was doing, though seeing her brought back my own memories of our hope-shattering day. To my surprise, I couldn't hold back my tears anymore. This time Kim bolstered me. "Sandy, your letter was a great encouragement. It came just when I needed it. Knowing you were praying for me was such a comfort."

I was comforted to know I had helped her, and I was glad to see how well she was doing. She had courageously faced her pain, and her example gave me strength. As I brushed away my tears, I knew it was finally time to deal with my grief from ministering to all the kids and parents after the tragedy. I'd gone to the luncheon thinking I could reach out to Kim, but God used her to reach out to me. She was the catalyst to my healing process.

Before that luncheon, the sound of police sirens or helicopters made me cringe because they reminded me of that day at Leawood. But now when I hear them, they remind me of

God's faithfulness and that He will provide me—and others—with the words and strength to do what He calls us to do.

*Names were changed to protect the "Thompsons'" privacy. Parts of this story appear in the book *Angry Kids and Parents Who Love Them* by Sandy Austin. This story has also appeared in *Teatime Stories for Women* and will appear in *Chicken Soup for the Christian Woman's Soul.*

PERFECT TIMING

by Rhonda Lane Phillips,
Blacksburg, Virginia

W e couldn't believe it. Every first day of school, for twenty years, the officials at Virginia Tech let our local Gideon camp distribute College Testaments—portions of the Bible—on the campus. But this year, for some odd reason, we'd not received permission. We wondered when, and if, we would be allowed to distribute these to the students.

We prayed that this door of opportunity for distributing God's Word would not be closed. We prayed that our Gideon husbands would receive this chance to witness through His Word and win the lost students to Jesus.

Finally, we received permission to distribute the green College Testaments on September 10 and 11. On September 10, few students visited the Gideon tent for a free Bible. Most walked on by. It looked like September 11 would be the same.

Then, it happened. . .the worst tragedy in United States history. As the events unfolded before students' eyes, many started to question their mortality. The pace stepped up in the Gideon tent. More and more students arrived to get their free Bibles. Many students who received testaments made a U-Turn that day, forever changed.

The Gideons distributed thirty-five hundred Scriptures on campus—most of them on the second day. God's timing is perfect. Surely He closed the door in August and opened it on September 11. He knows the plans He has for us, even for delaying distribution of His Word to the students at Virginia Tech.

Esther 4:14 reads, "For such a time as this. . . ."

FINDING STRENGTH

by Margo Dill,
St. Charles, Missouri

M om once said, "I'll never forget what I was doing when I heard President Kennedy was shot." My father felt that way about Elvis's death, my grandfather about Pearl Harbor. After September 11, I understood what they meant.

I was waiting for my fifth graders to return from recess when a colleague told me of the terrorists' acts. I was glad we had a teachers' meeting that afternoon so students would go home and I wouldn't have to reveal the news to them.

That night I sat glued to my television. I asked God to comfort the victims' loved ones and prayed that school would be canceled the next day. How could I teach math and reading after this? But then the principal called, not to cancel school, but to tell me to attend an early faculty meeting with our school counselor.

The next morning I got ready for school with knots twisting my stomach. At the faculty meeting, our counselor said, "You need to address yesterday's events with your students. I will give you some hints on how to start conversation, and I will be available if anyone cannot handle a situation."

A lump formed in my throat as I listened. When the bell rang, I left the meeting feeling dread. I reached the classroom door and prayed for strength and guidance. I often said that prayer, but this time it wasn't because I lost my patience with Billy or needed to call a parent. My country had been attacked. And I had no answers.

The students silently entered the room. After I took attendance, my stomach lurched as I asked, "Can anyone tell me something they know about yesterday?" Hands shot up. Almost everyone shared stories they had heard. When they finished, I asked, "Does anyone have any questions?" Again, many hands were raised. Most showed the same fear I felt.

"What will we do if a plane crashes into our school?"

"When will my mom get to come home from California?"

Or the hardest to answer, "Why do they hate us?"

I responded honestly, while twenty-six pairs of eyes stared at me. The mood in the room changed as the nervousness vanished. I reassured them that our nation stood ready. The counselor stuck his head in and asked, "Is everything going okay?"

"Yes," I answered honestly. Amazingly, my knots and lump were gone. My students and I had worked through some of the pain together.

While the children were at recess, I thought of my earlier prayer and knew it was answered. God gave me strength and guidance to help my students through a difficult time. When I wanted to run and hide, I couldn't. I had to do my job. It wasn't a heroic job like that of East Coast firefighters and police. But it was important to twenty-seven Americans in the Midwest.

When anthrax was found, my students posed more questions. I discussed the issues with confidence, knowing my role and remembering the strength God provided.

I will never forget hearing the news of the planes crashing. But most importantly, I will never forget the strength I received from a God who answers prayers.

LOVE ONE ANOTHER

Above all, love each other deeply,
because love covers over a multitude of sins.

1 PETER 4:8

THE PRAIRIE DWELLERS

by Lydia S. Ure, Ontario, Canada,
as told by Reverend Whiting

The beginning of my ministry coincided with one of the hardest times in American history. These were the toughest and best years of my life. On May 1929 I traveled west by train to my first pastorate. I was eighteen, dressed in my new grey suit and with most of my belongings in my dad's suitcase. I planned to evangelize everyone I met across the prairies. Some of my friends were being sent to city churches and would be paid well. But I would preach in farming communities and had no idea what my wages would be.

My elder met me at the station in a Model T. For the Prairie Dwellers, as the farmers were called, this would be a hard decade. From 1929 until 1939 no rain would fall, with the drought complicating problems of the Great Depression. We would not get out of this crisis until World War II (1939–1945) brought jobs.

Millions of acres of land became a wasteland with thousands of people leaving behind everything they owned. When the drought hit, the earth turned to dust and dust storms filled the air. Dust covered everything inside homes, and you could taste the grit in your mouth.

The drought affected twenty-seven states. The Dust Bowl area included parts of Colorado, Kansas, New Mexico, Texas, and Oklahoma. With no crops to sell, families went to bed hungry. Some nights I did too, but people shared what they had. One woman in her seventies, dressed in a faded housedress, would bring ten cents' worth of sugar in a little brown bag and drop it into the collection plate. Another woman told me, "I have six in my family, and my share is two turnips. Here's half of one of my turnips." She wrapped this in newspaper and handed it to me. I cooked it for dinner that day.

Many times my parishioners would invite me for dinner, but sometimes I refused because I knew they had so little and would go hungry.

One rancher, Clarence, walked six miles to attend a prayer service. When he learned I was taking on another school church, he said, "It will take some money, and they can't pay you. I was going to buy some boots when I sold my thirty-eight bushels of oats, but I'll give you the money."

A few days later, Clarence sold his oats. "Here," he said, handing me his money. "You do what God wants you to do. I kin get other things for my boots."

I didn't want to take it, but I knew a refusal would offend him. He wanted to do this to further the Lord's work. That Sunday as I preached, Clarence sat in his usual place up front. He had tacked pork rind on the worn soles of his boots. There he sat with flies zooming around his feet. But that was Clarence, a loving, faithful man of God.

In l935 the federal government formed a Drought Relief Service and eventually provided $525 million for drought relief. The rains finally came in l939 and ended the ten-year drought.

After fourteen years of ministry in the prairies, I left with my wife and two children for Pontiac, Michigan, with a greater understanding of faithfulness, sacrifice, compassion, and love. I had watched farms turned into a wasteland, but had seen souls filled with the Holy Spirit. The Prairie Dwellers, the prairies, are a part of me now. I will always remember those American Moments as the best of times.

CIVIL WAR FRIENDS

by Margaret Sayler,
Sacramento, California

The Doan family crossed the Missouri creek with aching feet and exhausted bodies. Their journey from Illinois with three wagons had been long. As they approached the large farmhouse, they hoped the owners would put them up for the night.

"Put your horses and wagons in our barn, then join us for dinner," the farmer warmly welcomed them.

Inside the house, ten-year-old Julius smelled the roast pork and saw extended tables heaped with food for the farmer, his family, hired help, and the Doans. After the blessing, everyone ate generous portions of meat, mashed potatoes, corn, biscuits, and apple pan dowdy.

The farmer looked around at the six sons and two daughters of Joseph and Anna Doan.

"My family is smaller than yours," he said. "But I have another son. During the war he was a captain for the Confederates. We expect him momentarily."

Julius choked. He looked at John and Jessie, his two older brothers, who had just returned from the Civil War. John had even served under Union Commander General William T. Sherman. But now these Union men responded to the farmer's announcement with casual smiles, as if they considered Confederates friendly neighbors.

After dinner the family and guests settled in the front parlor where the farmer's daughters played the piano and sang. Normally Julius would have sneaked behind the piano and pulled the young soprano's pigtails, but tonight his stomach churned. When the farmer's son appeared, would there be a fight? Julius hated a showdown. He couldn't understand how the rest of the family kept their composure.

At last the front door opened. Surprisingly, John jumped to his feet. "Matthew!" John cried, his face beaming as the farmer's son entered the room.

"John!" the farmer's son, Matthew, exclaimed. He turned to his father and explained, "John rustled for Sherman's army on the march to Savannah! I was his prisoner."

Mouths flew open. For a moment everyone stared at the two men.

"You treated me well," the farmer's son told John. "We became good friends," he told his father.

Matthew and John shook hands. Julius heard the host family say, "John surely must have treated Matthew well!"

Julius settled back in his chair. He thought about the love his brothers had always shown him. Now he knew what made them so special. He often heard them pray, "God, let your Calvary love pour out through our lives." God had answered their prayers.

Remembering this story in later years stirred the heart of my grandfather, Julius. God's great love brought Jesus from the splendor of heaven to pay a devastating price for the world's sin. Anticipating the time when he would see Jesus, Julius knew he would marvel at what Jesus did. This gave him confidence to believe God readily answers our prayers.

As Matthew sat down, surrounded by his family and the Doans, an impish smile lit young Julius's face. He decided if that girl sang again, he'd find a way to steal over and pull her hair.

GRACE LAKE

by Kathleen Coudle King,
Grand Forks, North Dakota

t's coming! The water's on Twentieth Street! Leave!" After
shouting his message, the driver of the car peeled off, leaving me feeling as if I were in some kind of doomsday
movie.

With the snowmelt of seven blizzards, the Red River had
been rising steadily. Our home in Grand Forks, North Dakota,
was on the border of the flood plain. In the last flood, twenty
years earlier, our house had not even gotten water in the
basement. So my husband, Alan, and I had moved a few
items upstairs and prepared to stick out the flood with our
three-year-old son and one-year-old daughter.

The air raid sirens, which had sounded for the last two
nights calling people to evacuate other areas of town, now
sounded again. The Emergency Alert System on the TV
beeped and a woman's trembling voice reported, "This is the
911 operator. The dike at Sherlock Park has been breached.
Please evacuate." The emotion in her voice chilled me. The
911 operator wasn't supposed to cry!

When we learned the water would be shut off, Alan and
I knew we couldn't manage two children in a home without
electricity or water. But the seriousness of the matter had not
yet sunk in. We threw some clothes together, planning to vacation in Montana for a week. That should be enough time
for things to get back to normal.

An hour into our sojourn west, the radio station announced chilling events. A building downtown had caught

on fire. Firefighters couldn't get trucks into the area because of flood water. Many buildings were destroyed before the fires were controlled.

We finally stopped for the night. Here we saw God's grace through the generosity of his people. Hotel managers were giving evacuees discounted rooms.

Alan and I reconsidered our plans as we watched the flood on the national news. We decided to find a cabin closer to home in Bemidji, Minnesota, where we could stay until we could get back home to clean up.

So the next morning, we headed back toward home. It took all day to reach our destination because of detours— our community wasn't the only one flooding. Late that night we pulled into a lakeside resort. We moved into a suite with a beautiful view of Lake Bemidji, thinking we'd only be there a week. Residents of Bemidji were amazing. They set up centers to provide flood evacuees with tetanus shots, food, a message center, free newspapers, clothes, and even rolls of quarters for laundry.

After we had been in our cabin a week, neighbors from Grand Forks called us. They knew someone who wanted to lend a cabin to flood evacuees. Could we use it? Could we ever! The space we were in was getting too expensive and too small. We arrived at the cabin and were not too surprised that it sat on "Grace Lake." Grace is exactly what we felt.

In the midst of this natural disaster, we were basking in God's grace. Everywhere we turned people extended kindness. When money ran low, I went to a food cupboard for the first time in my life. No one wants to ask for help; however, at times God permits U-Turns in our lives so we can see others' goodness.

I selected some peanut butter and diapers, avoiding

"luxury" items. A young man working there had other ideas. He began putting food in a paper bag. "I'm sure your kids would like some cookies. And you'll need bread and. . . ." He filled two bags. I couldn't talk because of the lump in my throat.

We could finally check our home nine days after we had evacuated. We had no first floor damage, but our basement was another matter. After seeing the water filling the basement, we went to the lower level entrance outside and opened the door. Stale, dirty water flooded out of the laundry room.

The washer and dryer were away from the wall at odd angles. The sofa and chair in the family room were on their backs. My oak rolltop desk was on its back, its thirty-four drawers with brass knobs swollen shut, the contents muck within. The room where we kept our books was down a level, and the water was still waist high, with books floating in the beam of my flashlight. The brass canopy bed in the guest room ended up mangled from thrashing in the water. I could not envision what it must have been like when the river filled my house. Clearly, it hadn't been a slow fill, but something violent and fast. Our work was cut out for us.

Back at Grace Lake, I watched the children while Alan drove the three hours home and began pumping the seven feet of water out of our basement. Most of what was precious to me did not survive the flood.

One of the most powerful lessons I learned from the flood was just how much goodness is in the world. When you least expect it, I hope that you too will receive a U-Turn and discover that life has given you a moment of God's grace.

SCHOOLROOM LESSONS IN LOVE

by Joyce Anne Munn,
Watts, Oklahoma

My hand flew to my mouth and I gasped. The newscaster had announced the bombing of our marine base in Lebanon. My concern was more than general outrage. I wondered what questions I would answer in the next few hours. I begged God for strength.

It was in October 1983, and I taught fourth graders. Days earlier, our class had located Lebanon on a map and discussed our troops. A student's brother was a marine at that base. How proud Kenneth was of his brother.

At school, I breathed a prayer for wisdom. When Kenneth entered the room, I glanced around. Most youngsters continued their activities. Expressions on a few faces, however, told me they knew what had happened. Kenneth walked to his desk and put his head down. I walked over and stooped down. I don't remember what I said. But the little boy raised his head and stared at me. His eyes held a depth of pain I had seldom seen. Abruptly, he put his head back on his desk.

When we stood for the flag salute, my voice trembled so that I could only whisper the words. I sent Kenneth to the office with the lunch count. While he was gone, I told the kids what little I knew from those first news reports of the bombings. Several children had questions, but I had few answers. How do you explain a terrorist attack?

How should we react to Kenneth? I suggested that the children do only what they felt comfortable doing or saying. I didn't want twenty-five students hovering over him saying inappropriate things, nor did I want them ignoring him out of confusion. I suggested they include him in activities, but leave him alone if he wanted to be by himself.

This first morning after the tragedy, families did not yet know about their loved ones' status. I told the children that it might be a day or more before relatives received any news. As it turned out, it took several weeks. Kenneth's brother was the next to the last lifeless body identified.

The children handled the situation well. They talked to Kenneth but had an extraordinary sense of when he needed time alone. Frequently, I noticed someone pat him on the shoulder while passing his desk. Some told me they were praying for him.

During Christmas break, more than two months after the bombing, the young marine's body was returned home. The burial took place on a cold, blustery day. A few students were present with their parents. My body shook as the marines gave their final gun salute.

School resumed in January, and I hoped to get back to normal. Kenneth returned to childhood activities, but I felt an overwhelming sense of seriousness not usually found in a fourth-grade class. We still laughed, but little things took on new significance. When a student was absent, children expressed concern. If someone got hurt on the playground, others quickly offered assistance. There seemed to be fewer quarrels and more willingness to share. It was as though these young hearts had all made subtle U-Turns toward loving one another.

Then came the day when our children's news publication contained a story for discussion and a picture of the barracks in Lebanon. I offered Kenneth the choice to stay for the discussion or go to the library. To my relief, he chose the library. Class discussion ran the gamut of emotions. We expressed anger, cried, questioned, voiced pride in our country, and cried some more. Eventually, we were calm, and Kenneth returned.

During February I always do a patriotic unit, which includes writing letters to the President. I explained to the children that they could write about whatever they wanted. Within minutes Kenneth asked if he really could write anything. I said yes, only making a stipulation that they had to be polite.

Later Kenneth handed me his letter. My tears flowed after school as I read his heart-wrenching words. Before mailing the letters to President Reagan, I attached a note explaining that Kenneth's brother was one of the last two marines identified.

A few weeks later, Kenneth came to school with a surprising announcement. He had received a letter from President Reagan.

"President Reagan said to thank you for your note." The next day Kenneth brought the letter. The President addressed the Lebanon tragedy, mentioning Kenneth's brother by name. He expressed his sympathy and promised his prayers. Then, sure enough, he sent regards to me with a thank-you for my note. I was impressed that our busy Executive Officer took a few moments to write to a distraught boy. We discussed the letter in class.

Several years have passed since that attack on our marines, but I still shudder when newscasts cover another bombing. Helen Keller once said, "Although the world is full of suffering, it is full also of the overcoming of it."

I pray a lot for my students. I pray that those youngsters, especially Kenneth, truly learned how to overcome in the face of tragedy and reach out to others. I pray they will each continue their own personal paths to understanding God's special plan for each of their lives.

ESCAPE FROM GROUND ZERO

by Lynn Roaten Terrell,
Wichita, Kansas

J eff was irritated. Once again, his newspaper was not
delivered.

"Don't worry," he murmured to himself. "The day has
to get better from here!"

As he rode the subway to his office in the Financial
District, he heard passengers discussing news that a plane
had just hit the World Trade Center.

"I wonder if we'll see it, if it's still sticking out of the
side?" asked one man.

Jeff wondered if a student pilot had veered out of the
flight pattern. Had something happened to the VOR—the
tracking system the airport uses to guide airplanes? And how
would that problem impact air traffic over the city? He figured historians would simply place a footnote on their cal-
endars, much like they did in 1945 when the Empire State
Building withstood the impact of a B-25 bomber.

By the time Jeff reached his exit, sirens screamed throughout Manhattan.

"Another plane struck!" a pedestrian shouted.

Jeff hurried the few remaining blocks to work and then
walked two blocks past work, standing across the street from
the World Trade Center. He watched as people rushed from
the towers. Some victims were carried out. Some fell from windows that exploded. People jumped out the windows to escape
the raging inferno.

About a half-hour later, Jeff returned to his office, which

overlooked the World Trade Center. Suddenly, a vibration rocked the plaza. Jeff stood transfixed as a gray cloud rose where walls of steel and concrete once stood. In a tragic American Moment, the great tower was instantly erased from Manhattan's skyline. Debris from the collapsing structure rushed toward Jeff.

In what he thought would be the last few seconds of life, he did a quick assessment. "I reviewed my life, and I was satisfied. I felt the presence of God, and I was at peace."

But as the dust cloud impacted his building, the structure held. He was alive. Turning from the window, he watched the television. It was surreal—observing the chaos from his window and watching it on TV at the same time.

"As the smoke cleared, I could see the street again. There were people covered in soot, wandering aimlessly in shock."

The second tower emerged from the cloud, and black smoke swirled from gaps in the seams. Would that tower hold?

"We sensed that it would also fall, but we couldn't do anything, so we just watched and waited," Jeff recalls.

It was like a movie. Only those were not actors—they were fathers, mothers, wives, husbands, brothers, and sisters. They were firemen, policemen, EMT personnel. They were victims.

"We've got to get out of here," someone said. Employees ran toward the exits. Suddenly, the second tower fell. The air was a deadly soup that did not clear up this time. They were trapped.

"It was amazing, but my father finally got a call through after the second tower fell. I told him to tell my mother I was fine, but that if something did happen to me, I was happy with my life and they should know I was okay to die."

Hours later the dust settled somewhat and Jeff left, his

face covered with wet napkins. He joined throngs of others hurrying north.

"The dust was over our ankles. I turned the corner, away from the soot," Jeff explains. "Suddenly, I had the best feeling I ever had. I nearly cried. I saw the Mom and Pop shops—that barely eked out an existence. Owners were bringing water and towels to the injured. Throughout those small communities like Chinatown and Little Italy, they had dragged tables and chairs onto the sidewalks and offered cool drinks to ash-covered pedestrians pouring into their neighborhoods from the Financial District. I was never so proud of New York as I was then."

When Jeff got home, he was deeply affected by the events. The visions of death were etched in his mind. It was a time to mourn.

"I have always been the type of person who has a zest for living. After September 11 that zest was enhanced. You can't experience something like this and not be affected," he muses.

His new office doesn't overlook the cleanup operations, and that helps the healing process. However, he is still disturbed when he hears discussions about petty irritations. "This event put life in perspective for me," he says. "What's the point in complaining about the little things? What purpose does it serve?

"New York went through an historic American Moment in time together. The U-Turn we made as a city can never truly be understood if you weren't here. We are all kinder to each other. The little things just don't matter anymore!"

He will never again say, when his newspaper is late, "The day has to get better from here!"

He knows, too well, that before the end of the day, he may have to stand before God and account for his life.

"I was ready to die that day, knowing I would go to heaven. Being able to say that gives me peace, and it's a peace I pray I can share with others when I talk about that moment in history."

RECOVERY AT GROUND ZERO

by Melissa Chavez,
Templeton, California

S tanding near the tip of Manhattan, I could finally gaze on Lady Liberty. Overcast skies couldn't obscure her beauty. As I walked through Battery Park, I watched a black man with graying hair sing: "God bless America, my home sweet home. . . ." A bucket at his feet welcomed tips, but he didn't sound as if he was singing for his supper. His tenor was heartfelt and insistent. I switched on my tape recorder so I could savor it again with my family in California.

As twilight approached, my friend Lisa and I grew colder and walked across the street for coffee. How odd it seemed, to be comforting myself on the way to Ground Zero.

Christmastime brought many visitors to the area. While those who worked the Financial District dashed from office buildings to catch buses and hail cabs, out-of-towners headed toward the sixteen-acre site of Ground Zero. Seven-foot fencing enclosed recovery efforts. Cranes continued deconstruction. We heard a constant roar and beeping of trucks, and bright lights illuminated the darkest crevices.

We approached St. Paul's Chapel at Broadway and Fulton Streets where wrought-iron fencing supported children's drawings and personal offerings—shirts, toys, flowers, photos of loved ones, and handwritten Scripture. Candles were lit. Two young women signed a vinyl banner.

Wondering if the arrival of yet another tourist would be met with disdain, I was amazed at the kindness of NYPD officers, National Guards, and volunteers shielding the perimeter and answering visitors' continual questions. Men and women in boots and hard hats exited the chapel, their haven of quiet from the work site. A busload of Indiana college students gathered on the sidewalk. Soon, a heavenly chorus of Christmas carols echoed between tall buildings.

Working at one of the World Trade Center checkpoints, NYPD Officer John Knapp told us how public support has affirmed him and his coworkers. "Everyone has been much better to us since it happened—very generous. If you go to the church, you'll see letters from kids all over the world. At police headquarters, they hung them all over the walls. I have a bunch in my pocket, more in the car. I don't want to see them thrown away." Boxes of Christmas ornaments made by children worldwide wait at St. Paul's.

"They'll be on my tree this year," John continued.

The events of September 11 were a wakeup call to John to begin thinking about the brevity of life. "I think about what kind of person I am, what I can do to help people. People all day long say, 'Thank you.' 'Can I get you a cup of coffee, buy you something?' The volunteers, the donations. . . they don't have to do that. Kids don't have to write letters and people don't have to feed us, but they do."

He worked twenty- or thirty-hour shifts during the first few weeks after September 11. Other police officers came from all over the country on their own time. As the winter melted into spring, Officer Knapp kept working double shifts. Funerals of fellow officers were hard to bear.

National Guard Specialist John Hall, a soft-spoken forty-year-old Brooklyn resident, now finds he appreciates relationships more. "I look at how these people—on a normal, beautiful day—went to work and look at what happened," John recalled. "A lot of kids' parents didn't come home. It has helped me love people more because you never know when you're going to leave. I live one day at a time, try to live the best I can and treat people the way I would like to be treated."

How has he explained the attacks to his daughter, eleven, and son, six, and reconciled their fears about their father working at the site? "This was not an act of God. These were evil people who committed a sin. I always tell [my children] that God will protect them, so they have nothing to worry about. I was brought up a Christian. I always believed in God because of the miracles He did in my life. That's helping me cope with this."

Three young firemen from the San Jose Fire Department arrived to visit the site, where they told about triumphs they've experienced since September 11.

"It's brought us closer together as a fire department," says Mario Minoia. "Every firefighter who used to bicker about little things; well, that doesn't matter anymore. We've gotten closer, and we've come here to pay our respects, kind of like a pilgrimage."

"We come here, meet the guys from New York, and they take us in as one of their own," Brian Demare explains.

Recovery at Ground Zero goes beyond physical unearthing, compelling us to consider a greater purpose. Some people reevaluate their values. Faith has become deeper, more important.

September 11 undeniably confirmed that at a moment's notice, thousands of people from all walks found one desire greater than all others—to love their neighbors more than their own lives. Scripture reads, "Greater love hath no man than this, that a man lay down his life for his friends" (John 15:13 KJV).

A slightly different version appeared in three parts in *Paso Robles Magazine,* February, March, and April 2002.

WE ARE ALL COLUMBINE

by Trina Lambert,
Englewood, Colorado

started praying when I learned a boy had brought a gun to the middle school four blocks from my home—the school my children would attend in three years.

This occurred after the event at Columbine, which was only twenty minutes from my home. Then I'd heard the sirens screaming toward the local hospital. But this time it was closer to home. We used to think that these things only happened to other people's children—children who lived far from us, children of a different income bracket, or children in large cities. But we now know the boy or girl next door could be the one we must fear. In that sense, we are all Columbine.

After Columbine, I tried to understand what adults could do differently so today's seven year olds would not become tomorrow's Columbine students—neither killers nor victims. Then I dreamed I saw Eric Harris and Dylan Klebold before their killing spree. I tried to change their plans with kind words. I ended up crouching under the tables, waiting for them to decide who would live, die, or be injured. I had no power over my children's safety. I heard the guns of the killers. Heat radiated throughout my body as I waited and prayed. After Harris spared my children, he pointed the gun at me.

Mercifully, I awoke. But. . .did God speak to me through that dream? Do I have the power to protect my children and those around me after all?

I experienced a U-Turn in my life. As my children grow

older I have now stayed involved with their school. I go on field trips, attend classroom parties, and call my children's classmates by name. Sometimes I have to remind myself to be friendly with kids who seem to cause trouble. Maybe they need a little more encouragement and a lot less judgment.

Perhaps others in my community feel the same way. School administrators are offering programs about how to treat others. Some doctors have adopted our school; more retired people share their time. People who have no ties to the school make a statement to the kids through their presence. The volunteers show our children that people care about them—including people who aren't paid to be there.

We cannot transform a society overnight. Yet, we are not helpless either. God calls us to make a positive difference in the lives of our children. This is reflected in our schools, neighborhoods, homes, and in the behavior we model to the world. We can choose to live by the Golden Rule. We can choose to make a U-Turn toward God in the way we live our lives.

Jesus tells us in Mark 12:28–31 that the two greatest commandments are to love the Lord our God with all our hearts and to love our neighbors as ourselves. We put our love for Him into action by getting to know our neighbors' children, by showing them we think they are important, and by not tolerating bullying.

We are, after all, all Columbine. Next time, the announcer may mention the school down the road from you. Or maybe not—because of how you changed your world.

A REMINDER TO LOVE

by Grace M. Graziano,
Orlando, Florida

One advantage of living in Satellite Beach, Florida, south of Cape Kennedy, is seeing Cape Kennedy liftoffs first-hand from our doors, windows, or the beach.

The flight on January 26, 1986, was heavily publicized since Christa McAuliffe, a civilian teacher, would be on this flight. When it was time for the liftoff, my coworkers and I walked across the street to the beach to witness another spectacular venture into space. The liftoff went well, but moments later we saw a strange billowing we hadn't seen before. The *Challenger* had exploded. Oh no, it can't be. I didn't witness that. God, please let this be a mistake.

For many days after that, I pondered, Why did this happen, God? Why would You let that happen to seven innocent people who worked so hard to prepare for this flight?

I didn't get my answer then. I probably wouldn't have heard it anyway, because I was too angry. Not until many years later did I understand there is a time and season for everything and that God is the only one in control. As we learn to trust God and keep the faith He wants us to have, we must focus less on the questions and ask Him to hold our hands in crises.

The world watched with horror as seven lives ended that January day. I believe it was an American Moment wakeup call to remind us to show our love for one another, to see how short life can be, and to say all the kind and loving words we often keep hidden. May we all learn to listen to our sovereign God better. Accepting what enters our path is sometimes difficult, but God's love will get us through. He knows the plans He has for us and will work everything out for our good. He promised that, and He never fails us.

WHEN THE WORLD BECAME ONE

by Norka Blackman-Richards,
Rosedale, New York

T he United States was a long way from Panama City as we dashed to the airport to return home to New York that day. Before leaving my parents' house that morning, I saw the airplane crash into one of the WTC towers on television. But we didn't grasp the impact of what we saw. We were too involved in packing and saying good-bye. My mother dropped us off at the airport and went on to her job teaching English at a prominent high school.

We checked our luggage while hearing pieces of information: "Terrorist attack on the United States." "Airports closed." "Airplanes used as missiles." The atmosphere was tense as airport security crowded the lobby. Bomb-squad units and dogs pushed through the nervous crowd. I called my mother. Her voice was agitated. "This is pandemonium! Students are crying and parents are crowding into the classrooms and grabbing their children."

We were assured it was safe to board our flight. I started to pray. "Dear Lord, if it is not Your will and our lives will be in any type of danger, let our feet not leave Panama today." Then airport officials announced: "No one traveling to the United States can leave today. There has been a terrorist attack on the United States, and air space is closed."

After waiting for hours for our suitcases, we returned to my parents' home. We watched the reports on TV in horror. Tears filled our eyes as we heard of the death totals.

We contacted a leader in our church. We had been

assigned to the New York congregation in March 1999. Many members of our church worked in or near the Towers. We learned that our sound technician, who worked in one of the Towers, was missing. We felt powerless. It was disastrous that as the ministerial couple we could not be there to comfort his family and the congregation. How we longed to minister to our brothers and sisters and pray with them. We needed to get home. We felt that no one in Panama could understand our pain.

Soon we realized how wrong we were. America's pain had become the world's pain. These heinous crimes had not only touched one of the world's super powers, but also had touched every human in some way. Friends, even strangers, called my parents' home to check on us and offer words of comfort. Although many of these people had never been to the United States, they felt our pain. Churches in Panama held prayer vigils for our church family and the American people. Memorials were erected throughout the city with roses, teddy bears, white sheets, handkerchiefs, notes, and Panamanian and American flags of all sizes. Schoolchildren and adults left testimony of their solidarity.

The world's outpouring of sympathy was overwhelming. We cried as we learned of the memorials in diverse parts of the world. The poorest nations and the wealthiest super powers had become one. The pain of the mothers, fathers, husbands, wives, and children became the pain of the world. The brave rescue workers on Ground Zero became the world's heroes. The energetic appeal of the U.S. President and Congress for the eradication of terrorism became the world's aim.

Perhaps more than any other American Moment, September 11 will be remembered as the day the world became one, making a collective U-Turn toward God as we prayed and mourned together.

THE UNIVERSAL LANGUAGE

by Tony Gilbert,
Albany, Georgia

was in heaven when Georgia hosted the Summer Olympics in 1996. Ever since I was thirteen years old, I had been an Olympic fanatic. My athletic ability (or inability) would never give me the chance to compete, but I was selected as an official for the track and field venue.

Although I could see the Games from the inside, I wasn't about to miss the revelry available to spectators—even if it just meant standing on a street corner watching the crowds. The whole city offered diversions, but entertainment in Centennial Olympic Park was a cultural extravaganza. Thousands of guests from other countries gathered in the name of peace, harmony, and fun. Centennial Olympic Park was a people watcher's paradise.

Despite spending most of my time in the park that week, my early-bird habits brought me back to our Emory University dorm at a decent hour each evening. That would change on Friday, the first night of track and field competition.

That night, I was officiating the opening round of the men's triple jump. Our event ended about the time I would normally be leaving Centennial Olympic Park. I planned to take a bus back to the dorm, drive into the city, and enjoy the park into the early hours, since I had no duties the next morning.

Boarding the bus behind the stadium, I took off my blazer and pulled down a window. Other officials came aboard, and the bus filled with passengers. Suddenly, "The

Star-Spangled Banner" filtered from the stadium and into the open bus windows. Everyone reverently listened as it echoed throughout the evening air. We all knew what it meant. An American had won gold in the shot put, the first event to award medals. No one spoke again as the bus pulled away moments later. Everyone was overcome with emotion, pride, and patriotism.

On the way to the dorm, my plans changed. Nothing in Centennial Park could top that. I wanted the highlight of our National Anthem echoing through the night air to be my final memory of that night, so I went straight to bed.

That night a bomb had exploded in the park just when I'd planned to be there. Two people were dead and dozens injured. I was immediately awake. If I hadn't heard the national anthem echoing inside the bus, I would have been in the park when the bomb exploded.

The next morning I watched SWAT teams investigate the desolate park, which would otherwise be teeming with thousands of visitors. The Olympics took on a more somber mood for three days as the park was closed. The park had been the symbol of these Games, a place for people of the world to gather.

When the gates reopened Tuesday morning, I waited among the thousands. The masses outside the park were more diverse than before. As I glanced around the crowd, I thought of the words to that simple song, "Red or yellow, black or white, they are precious in His sight. Jesus loves the little children of the world."

We are all His children, I realized, and here we were, with our different colors, costumes, and languages, to renew a spirit that had been lost a few days earlier. A group of Asian students began to sing softly. I knew the tune and joined in my own language, as did most others.

United by the universal language of music and love, we entered the gates while in various tongues we sang, "Mine eyes have seen the glory of the coming of the Lord. . . ."

TRIUMPH OVER TRAGEDY

by Kristine Vick,
Columbia, South Carolina

I hung up the phone and immediately arranged to fly halfway across the country. My editor had just told me about the Columbine shooting. In eight years of reporting for CBN News, I had covered several school shootings, but nothing could prepare me for this.

When I arrived, the park outside the school grounds was already a makeshift memorial. Flowers, stuffed animals, candles, and letters lined the fences and lawn. People of all ages stood with bewilderment. Many were sobbing. Teens held hands, singing "Amazing Grace." A man was preaching an impromptu sermon to some kids about forgiveness.

This was the first day of nearly two weeks I would spend in Littleton, but already I sensed that God was in the midst of this tragedy. Perhaps Colorado Governor Bill Owens said it best the next day in our interview, "Maybe God is working here in His mysterious ways."

Mysterious because no one can explain why God would allow such a thing. Yet, anyone in that community can tell you they felt a clear sense of His presence, His grace, and His love.

I felt it when I interviewed the family of Rachel Scott, a junior who was killed. I felt it when I sat with Kacey Ruegsegger as she described being shot while hiding under a computer table. I felt it when John Tomlin's parents recounted the last words they shared with their son at the breakfast table. And, I felt it when I saw seventy thousand people gather at a memorial service for the victims a week later. When the crowd proudly chanted, "We Are Columbine," a lump in my throat burned.

In this American Moment in time, evil evidently would not prevail in Littleton, Colorado. As an entire community turned toward God, and a country shared its grief and pain, it became clear that God's love would triumph. As it always does.

PRIDE AND PREJUDICE

by Lynn Roaten Terrell,
Wichita, Kansas

I cranked open the little side window in the front seat and savored the fresh air blowing onto my warm cheeks. The front seat was usually reserved for grownups. If no other adults were in the car, my seven-year-old brother got to ride up front with Mamma. But today, it was just Mamma and me in the car. I felt very special.

I watched out the little window as we sped from the relative prosperity of Southern Tennessee to the hovelled communities of Northern Mississippi. We soon pulled into a driveway—a path, really—that led to an unpainted shack. A yard full of laughing children with beautiful dark golden skin and curly ribboned hair scampered to greet us. A cute little girl was even wearing a blouse like I used to have. I was sure we would find lots more in common if we were given the chance to talk.

I ached to jump out of the car and play with them. But then my heart raced with excitement as my special friend, LoAnna, kissed them all good-bye and hurried toward our car.

Usually, she rode the bus in; but today we got to pick her up. She often fixed soup and grilled-cheese sandwiches for my brother and me for lunch, and patiently cared for our baby sister. One time, using a hoe, she fought off a nest of lizards she found behind my brother's bed. She didn't complain when the bird egg broke in my sun-suit pocket. LoAnna even let me play in the doghouse with our beagle, and she generously warned me three times before turning my many misdeeds over to my mother for discipline. She was the only grownup I was allowed to call by her first name.

As LoAnna joined us, I scrambled into the back seat, following the family rule that adults always sat up front. LoAnna stood awkwardly, as my mother caught my eye.

"You need to get back here in the front seat with me," she ordered.

"You mean in the front seat with the two of you?" I was sure I had heard wrong.

"No, up front. . .just with me."

LoAnna smiled her gentle, knowing smile as she nodded her okay. Confused, I crawled out of the back of the car. I held the seat forward for her, as she nestled herself amid the Popsicle sticks and apple cores that garnished the back seat.

I didn't understand. Mamma thought LoAnna was good enough to care for her children. So, I couldn't figure out whether Mamma thought LoAnna wasn't smart enough to be around grownups, or if LoAnna might have done something wrong and wasn't allowed to sit up front.

I will never forget the ride home. I was humiliated by the fact that I, a child, had taken the place of honor away from a grownup who had earned my utmost love and respect—for a few dollars a day, plus bus fare. As punishment, I closed the little side window that gave me such joy. The front seat had abruptly lost its allure. It was years before I understood this event.

That was 1955. During the sixties, I was protected from much of the racial turmoil as I attended a small college in Northern Mississippi. As Easter 1968 approached, I looked forward to relaxing at my grandparents' house in my hometown. Then, just before I was to leave, an intense emotion filled the air at my college.

"What's all the excitement about?" I asked my friends, as we sat in the auditorium for the chapel service.

"Dr. Martin Luther King, Jr., was assassinated in Memphis. I hear they're sending riot squads to control the protesters."

The dean took the podium. "I am sure you have all heard about the shooting of Dr. Martin Luther King, Jr. Most of you have to travel to Memphis this week, but curfews are in place due to rioting. As you know, the campus is usually closed over Easter," he continued.

"I'll bet they cancel our holiday." I moaned.

"So, if any of you are afraid to go home, we will let you stay in the dorms."

Despite the warning, I caught the bus. Passengers discussed the shooting until the bus picked up passengers at the black college. After that, we rode in palpable silence.

When my grandfather picked me up at the bus stop, I didn't recognize the city I loved. The odor of burning trash hung in the air as protesters lit garbage dumps. And Memphis, once a clean city, was now strewn with rusting garbage cans overflowing with rotting food.

My uncle, who worked for the city, was assigned to guard a landfill. After curfew began for the city—and armed with a pass from the mayor's office—my aunt and I took dinner to him. We visited for several hours—hours that were palpable with the textures of fear.

Although it seems like only yesterday, a lot has changed since then. Cars no longer have those wonderful little side windows. Adults ride in the front seat and children sit in the back, secured by seatbelts.

Prejudice has existed since the beginning of time, and as long as we have sinful natures, diversity will exist. Yet it is possible to make a U-Turn toward God when we fill our hearts with God's love—a love that knows no color, no race, no creed. We have turned the corner toward change, but still have a long way to go.

Because of those changes, children will never again have to try to analyze the parsed words of grownups as they're ordered to give their seats in the back to an adult. I didn't understand it then; and now, more than forty years later, I still don't understand it. Yet I will press onward and pray that in time our nation will be able to understand that powerful message of hope and healing that comes from treating hatred with love.

GOD ALLOWS U-TURNS®

FAITH

Faith is being sure of what we hope for
and certain of what we do not see.
HEBREWS 11:1

THE GREATEST SOLDIER OF ALL

by Patty Smith Hall,
Hiram, Georgia

I saw him staring at me. He was a simple man. Sprigs of snowy white hair peeked out from beneath a dirty ball cap, framing a wrinkled face that had weathered a lifetime of storms. Wearing worn blue jeans and a button-up shirt that had seen better days, he was probably someone's father or grandfather, stopping in the magazine aisle for the newest puzzle books. But right now, he was staring at what I had in my hands. A photo essay on Pearl Harbor.

Being a child of the 1960s, the surprise attack that had drawn the United States into World War II was just a history lesson to me. But in this man's eyes, I saw memories of a time and place so real I could have reached out and touched them. I had to talk to him.

"Nice book, isn't it?" I opened the ensuing conversation.

The muscles in his throat moved and for one brief moment, I felt ashamed for disturbing him. Then he spoke.

"I was there." Not for the attack, he added. He was a boy of eleven or twelve when the Japanese bombed Hawaii. He remembered the call to arms. The boys of Paulding County bravely marching to war. Stars hung in the windows of those who didn't make it back.

It affected him, and nine years later, he decided to join the marines. He shyly glanced at me. "I'd always been in church, saved when I was young boy. But the service changed me, and I slid away from the Lord. Until I got to 'Pearl.' "

His orders came in. After a brief layover in Hawaii, he

was being shipped to Korea to fight in a new conflict. Scared about what lay ahead, he decided to go see Battleship Row, particularly the entombed *Arizona*. Standing where so many had died, he watched as the infamous drops of oil rose to the surface. So many lives lost for the sake of freedom.

"And then, the Lord spoke to me in a quiet, still voice," he said. "He reminded me that one day the oil would run out and people could forget what happened there. But His Son shed drops of blood for my freedom that will last for all eternity."

The man gave his life back to the Lord that day, sure that no matter what happened in Korea, his everlasting freedom was secure. The old man shyly tipped his cap and shuffled away.

A lump formed in my throat as I gazed at the book in my hands, my fingertips caressing the laminated cover. So many young lives lost for the cause of freedom. One battle fought for our eternal deliverance. The nameless man had changed my textbook view of Pearl Harbor. Never again would it be just another documentary on the History Channel, but a constant reminder to give thanks for the men and women who serve our country every day. And to give wholehearted praise to the loving Warrior who battled the gates of hell to ensure my liberty from death.

For Christ truly is the greatest Soldier of all.

FAITH IN A FOXHOLE

by Tamara Swinson,
Tulsa, Oklahoma

D ean couldn't believe the terror around him when he arrived in Okinawa. With rockets on one shoulder and a bazooka on his other, he fled to the nearest foxhole. Lifeless bodies lay everywhere. Most were members of Bonsai and the Kamikaze—suicide groups who would get drunk on saki and shoot as many rounds of ammunition at Americans as they could before they were wounded enough to die.

Dean had already experienced much in his nineteen years. Two years earlier, he had married Betsy. Now, he thought of her every day as he huddled in a foxhole. Betsy was his high school sweetheart, and he knew their love would last forever. He wrote to her every day. This day, though, the day after he'd arrived on Okinawa, was different.

"I was shot up here," he said, pointing to his hip. "[The bullet] went right into my bone."

A medic ran to him. The young private shouted, "Get down!" As the medic ducked, a bullet went through Dean's tattered, green uniform pocket. It miraculously missed flesh. The medic ran to safety, leaving Dean alone. Dean expected to die.

Suddenly the end of a rope landed near him and he heard someone calling, "Hey, can you hold on?" Dean grabbed the rope and was dragged ten feet into a foxhole.

"I prayed for what seemed like a long time. I don't remember what I said. . .just that I made a lot of promises,"

Dean laughs. The next thing he knew, after his one day in Okinawa, he was sent home to heal.

Although Dean can't remember the specific prayers, he knew God was there. "Yet it wasn't until years later that I understood how important God really was in the whole scheme of things," Dean says. "There is certainly no one reason why God allowed me to live that day. My life is about day-to-day contentment. It's about coming home and sharing life with Betsy, and then having three boys together. It's about spending time with my family and friends."

While Dean was at Okinawa, Betsy had knitted sweaters for the Red Cross as her way of "doing her part." Sixty years after returning from active duty in WWII, Dean still remembers what it was like to lie in a foxhole, bleeding and asking God to let him see his young wife again. And Dean can also still remember what it was to come home and see Betsy again.

Betsy places a lovely, box frame on the table. It displays Dean's badges of courage, honor, and commitment, his uniform pocket with the bullet hole, yellowed envelopes that once held letters he sent to his beloved, pins he received, and the bullet removed from Dean's hip.

For Betsy and Dean, the American Moment we know as World War II is a bittersweet time in their lives. It set the stage for the years that would follow as their love grew.

I can't help but wonder where I would be had Dean not lived, because Dean is my grandfather. His purpose, his U-Turn from certain death, was life. Because he was only nineteen when he served at Okinawa, he had no clue of the goodness a close relationship with God would bring to his life. Though he cried to God in desperation, he barely understood real faith back then. All he needed was "faith of a mustard seed," and that was apparently enough.

So, my grandpa is not a Nobel Prize winner. He is not rich or famous. But he embraces the assurance that God has always been there, and that because his life was spared, his relationship with his Father progresses even now. He and Betsy both realize that only by the grace of God can the three of us sit together, eating warm pecans from their tree. It is only by God's grace that he lived to tell the story of true faith and love in a foxhole.

BUILDING DREAMS ON SHAKY GROUND

by Kari West,
Pleasanton, California

I was carrying a pot of baked beans to a single-again bar-beque at church when I met Richard, but our year-long courtship that followed was no picnic. Shortly before Richard asked me to marry him, he learned he had a tumor behind his ear. Together, we leaned on God. While Richard underwent a risky eight-hour operation, I addressed wedding invitations in the hospital. The surgery left Richard with balance and hearing on only his right side, and an unexplained ringing in his deaf ear. Besides tolerating this constant internal noise, Richard had to relearn how to walk, drive, and ride a bicycle.

We held few illusions about riding into an exquisite sunset. Four days before we were married, the Loma Prieta earthquake shook the area, measuring 7.1 on the Richter scale. It knocked down San Francisco's Embarcadero, buckled the Bay Bridge, collapsed buildings, and halted the World Series game. For two days, my daughter and I lived without electricity.

Shipments into San Francisco were curtailed, including flower deliveries. When the lady creating my wedding bouquets told me this, I said, "Then we'll get a chrysanthemum plant at Safeway and whack off the flowers."

When the windows fell out of the hotel Richard and I had booked for our wedding night, and several guests called to say damages would prevent their attendance, we decided we'd settle for any available hotel room and went on with the ceremony.

Since then a lot more of my expectations have been jolted off their foundations. But I've unearthed a few truths along the way. Mainly, that loss is the risk we take for living and loving in an unstable, unpredictable world. I also see how earth-shattering situations we would never choose can open possibilities and guide us to a strength greater than ourselves.

I could not have coped with life's uncertainty without Jesus. The stability of God's unchanging love provided the bedrock foundation of my hopes, dreams—my very life. When massive forces work around me, bent on collapsing my faith and buckling my sanity, God never moves. He remains stable.

FROM FEAR TO FAITH

by Gail Schuit,
Lake Ariel, Pennsylvania

I was on edge when the phone rang at 7 A.M. on August 7. I've found early morning and late night calls usually mean trouble. This time the bad news heralded was that the American Embassy in Nairobi had just been bombed.

I was horrified when we turned on the TV and saw the devastation. Eight buildings were affected by the blast, one totally demolished. People were buried beneath the rubble. Smoke billowed from the charred remains of buses and cars. Men and women bled profusely.

But this tragedy was also personal. My daughter and I had come to America to visit family and friends. We'd left my husband and son behind at our mission station in Kenya.

Two days after the bombing, I still had not heard from my husband. He and my son had planned to be in Nairobi on the morning of the bombing and could have been passing the Embassy at the time of the blast. The verse God gave me was Psalm 46:1–2: "God is our refuge and strength, an ever-present help in trouble. Therefore we will not fear."

I finally learned my husband and son were safe. My U-Turn journey through this American Moment was the growing knowledge that God doesn't want me to live in fear of what might happen. Fear wastes energy and zaps joy. I can choose how I live. I can fear or trust God. The Embassy bombing reminded me that life is too uncertain to waste a single minute. So today I will savor my morning coffee, take the dog for a long walk, lift my face to the sun's warmth, and revel in God's love and the love of family and friends.

HE LOVED THAT TRUCK

by Kristine Vick,
Columbia, South Carolina

H
e loved that truck," is what most people say when they think of John Tomlin, a student shot and killed at Columbine High School. John drove a light brown, souped-up, old Chevy that was his pride and joy. His father says John saved his money for months to buy it and was constantly putting money into the old jalopy to keep it running.

The day of the shooting, John had a quick breakfast with his mom, exchanged a few jokes in the kitchen, and headed to school. As usual, he parked the truck and went to class. John was fatally shot a short time later.

John would never return to his beloved Chevy, but in the following days, hundreds of others did. People laid flowers, letters, cards, and other tokens of love on the truck. Cards were stuffed under the windshield wipers, tulips stuck in the door handles, and a pink pig in a leather jacket rested on top of the cab. And, if you peered in the windows, you couldn't help but notice John's Bible sitting on the passenger seat. It was a subtle but powerful testimony to John's faith in Jesus Christ.

Perhaps John left it there on purpose, perhaps not. Whatever the reason, that gesture spoke volumes to those who saw it, including his mother and father. They had wondered where John stood in his walk with the Lord. Seeing that Bible gave them the comfort they needed to cope with their son's tragic death.

Even in his death, John Tomlin was a witness for the Lord too. People who saw that Bible sitting on the front seat saw a lasting message of hope.

Now, when people think of John, they say, "He loved that truck, and he loved the Lord."

ALOFT AND AFRAID

by Lt. Col. Robert B. Robeson,
U.S. Army (Ret.), Lincoln, Nebraska

T he urgent helicopter medical evacuation occurred more
than three decades ago in Vietnam, but I often think of
that traumatic night in late March of 1970—especially
when it's rainy, foggy, and overcast. That night I learned
about the power of faith at three thousand feet.

Earlier that day, in the late afternoon, operations in-
formed me that my aircraft maintenance officer at Landing
Zone Hawk Hill, thirty-six miles south of Da Nang, had
requested another Bell UH-1H "Huey" helicopter. He was
experiencing sudden power losses and hearing "strange noises"
from the engine compartment. I alerted my crew and flew
out to evaluate the situation.

The engine problems couldn't have occurred at a worse
time. Already that month, the thirteen pilots in our unit had
been shot or downed in sixteen different helicopters. We'd
gone through our inventory of six authorized aircraft nearly
three times. Now we were down to two. Also, a storm system
enveloped the region, and it was nearing dusk when we arrived.

After talking to my maintenance officer, we decided to
switch aircraft. We would load his ailing helicopter with
patients for Da Nang and fly back below the cloud deck
before weather grounded us for the night.

While we started to load patients, an urgent mission was
called in. Three American infantrymen had been seriously
wounded. The field-site crew scrambled to evacuate them. I
couldn't leave now. If the infantrymen were brought back to

Hawk Hill alive, I would have to fly them to the hospital in Da Nang, or they probably wouldn't survive. The crew returned in less than thirty minutes. Two soldiers had sucking chest wounds and the third was wounded in the head and extremities. We watched as the doctors feverishly worked to stabilize them.

Outside, night had fallen, and a thick fog had rolled in. It was beginning to rain, and a heavy layer of low-lying clouds hung above the fog. I saw only two alternatives. I could ground my aircraft for the night because of the weather and engine problems—and probably doom these patients. Or I could take off and be picked up by radar for a ground controlled approach at Marble Mountain Airfield in Da Nang. In combat, as in many other areas of life, you don't always do what you want to do. You do what you must. Sometimes, when you most want not to go, you most have to go.

With rain dribbling from the bill of my baseball cap and down the back of my neck, I thought of Psalm 121:8 (KJV): "The Lord shall preserve thy going out and thy coming in." I knew this would be another "going out" time, like eight hundred similar missions I'd flown. Despite the rain and darkness, I decided to leave as soon as our patients were stabilized. The rest would be in God's hands.

Six hours later our patients were ready for evacuation. My decision to take a sick bird into fog, clouds, rain, and dead of night. . .with a rookie copilot. . .was a definite act of faith. I prayed for our safety and tiptoed into a heavy, cotton-wool mist that hung over the landing pad. At two hundred feet, the clouds swallowed us. As I scanned my instrument panel, we climbed to three thousand feet before breaking out on top.

I made initial radio contact with Marble Mountain Tower and was quickly switched to approach control.

"Dustoff Six-Zero-Five," the controller said, "turn left to a heading of three-five-zero, maintain VFR [visual flight rules] on top and three thousand. Squawk 2233."

My copilot dialed 2233 into our transponder, which transmits position identifying signals, and activated the "ident" switch. I flew toward Da Nang.

"Six-Zero-Five, be advised I have negative radar contact," the controller noted.

I was too stunned to reply. What do you mean you have negative contact?

"Turn right to zero-niner-zero and maintain three thousand," he continued.

I verified the correct transponder code and hit the "ident" switch myself. Another long silence.

"Six-Zero-Five, I still have negative contact. State your intentions," the controller requested.

Then I heard the "strange noises" coming from the engine compartment. I felt like a fool for having risked so much. We were somewhere over the South China Sea near the coastal town of Hoi. I didn't want to let down slowly over the ocean because of mountains rising from islands off the Vietnamese coast. I was quickly running out of options.

"Marble Approach," I replied, "we have engine problems, and three seriously wounded U.S. are aboard, so I recommend someone trying to find us on radar before it gets worse."

I offered another heartfelt prayer. I had nothing left to hang on to but the cyclic stick and a total faith I had in an all-knowing and all-seeing God. The controller's voice again broke the silence. "Six-Zero-Five, turn right to one-eight-zero, maintain three thousand."

I banked south, feeling alone and afraid for our patients who might not have much sand left in their hourglasses.

After another long pause I heard him say, "Sir, I have radar contact eighteen miles southeast."

For an aviator adrift above a sea of clouds with lives in the balance, hearing "negative contact" and "I have radar contact" is like the difference between a wet match and a flame thrower.

Looking back, although I felt alone, I wasn't. With God, all's well even when it appears it isn't. The answer to my prayers really came in the words of Mark 5:36 (TLB): "Don't be afraid. Just trust me." I did and He took care of the rest.

To this day, I don't know what happened to that radar or why our engine didn't self-destruct. But I am sure that with God, we can find strength to do anything. We need prayer and courage to use the knowledge, talents, and abilities that God has given us. If we do, He'll work out the details.

Previously printed in *Signs of the Times,* April 1995; *New Covenant,* February 1997; *Live,* July 5, 1998; *Holiness Today,* June 1999, and *The Vision* (Missouri), March 5, 2000.

MISS RALPH GOES TO WASHINGTON

by Mary Ralph Bradley,
Cottontown, Tennessee

Y es, you can go."
I couldn't believe it when my parents agreed to let me go. I was just eighteen, but I was adventurous. And now I was going to Washington, D.C., to work in the war effort.

Shortly after the war started, a government worker had visited the business school where my two sisters, my aunt, and I were learning secretarial skills. Aunt Eva signed up for military work. In two weeks she was gone and writing that we should come to help in the war effort. My two older sisters never considered leaving our Tennessee farm, but I jumped at the chance.

As I headed toward the U.S. Capitol, I was excited and terrified. Not only was it my first train ride, but it was also my first time to travel more than one hundred miles from home. Family and friends had offered blessings for God's guidance. *Will God take care of me?* I wondered. I had become a Christian when I was fourteen. I silently prayed as the train rolled over the tracks. *Somewhere,* I thought, *God is caring about my fears.*

The day after arriving, I was sent to a small, crowded room in a navy building to begin practicing what I had learned at school. In April we were sent to a huge building being built that was called the Pentagon. When completed it would have nearly eighteen miles of corridors, but would take only seven minutes to walk between any two points in the building.

Soon I was secretary to Lieutenant Colonel Red Reeder and Major Tom Clarkin in the Operations Division of the War Department. My bosses' kindness and my Aunt Eva's charity helped me endure those first few weeks of incredible homesickness. I could not call home because my folks had no phone, but we wrote each other often. I read my Bible daily, and my faith deepened as I saw God working in my life.

One June day in 1942 the head of our department, Major General Dwight D. Eisenhower, walked into our office. He said, "I want to tell all of you good-bye. I'm going out where the boys are. You'll have to take care of things here."

Then he turned to me, introduced himself, and held out his hand. "Miss Ralph," he said, eyeing my name badge, "keep things going." As if I could do anything—but what a story to tell my children and grandchildren!

God led me to Washington, I believe, to find my husband. When I met Lawrence, who worked for the FBI, I was hooked. He was the kindest man I'd ever met and a phenomenal Christian. Amazingly, we'd grown up twenty-five miles apart but had never met. In April 1943 we were married in my hometown church.

In 1952 our nation faced a presidential election with two excellent candidates, Adlai Stevensen and Dwight D. Eisenhower. Raised in a family of Yellow Dog Democrats (those who would vote Democratic even if a yellow dog was the candidate), I faced a serious decision. Did I dare vote Republican? I knew Adlai Stevenson would make a good president. I also knew that Eisenhower had helped "make the world safe for democracy." He was the man whose hand I'd shaken, and for whom I'd prayed all through the war.

Head held high, I left the voting booth, knowing I'd made the right choice. I'd voted my heart and experience over family tradition, though my Democrat parents almost disowned me. I was elated when Eisenhower won. I knew this man's quality, I knew prayers were constant on his behalf, and I knew that God truly had blessed America.

My great love and I had forty wonderful years together as Lawrence taught school and directed worship. Together we led many souls to Christ. At age sixty-two, he had a massive heart attack as he led the song "O Lord, Our Lord." God called him home to sing in heaven.

God has guided my life. He used an American Moment in time, World War II, to give me the courage to choose an uncommon path that led from Tennessee to Washington and back again. Just as God cared when I was riding that train so long ago, He has continually been faithful. And I have been faithful to Him, for He cares for me.

GOD
ALLOWS
U-TURNS®

NEW
PERSPECTIVES

Carry each other's burdens,
and in this way you will fulfill the law of Christ.
GALATIANS 6:2

FREEDOM MARCH

by LaRose Karr,
Sterling, Colorado

I never understood segregation as a child born in the Deep South. My family had black neighbors and friends; we hired black farm workers in the fall. I played with Negro children while our parents worked together. We had great fun tumbling in the cotton-filled wagons.

I had no clue that black people had to go to back entrances of restaurants to get their meals. Whites and blacks had separate drinking fountains. In the 1960s we watched President Kennedy's assassination on TV, and the Vietnam War on the six o'clock news. The Beatles exploded on the Ed Sullivan Show. Hippies demonstrated against the war while their high school buddies died in Vietnam. Our nation was changing and tensions escalated.

But rural America was still quiet the day my dad, brother, and I were traveling from Arkansas to Georgia on vacation. Weary from the sweltering heat, we perked up when we saw a parade of black and white people walking down the roadside. Dad slowed his truck to a crawl, and my brother and I watched the determined faces. I didn't realize the significance, but we were watching a Martin Luther King Freedom March.

I had to grow up before I could appreciate that scene. Today I know bondage is a tool of Satan and takes many forms: physical and emotional abuse, alcoholism, drug addiction, unfair employment practices. I understand that only Jesus can set us free from those chains. And I pray we have the courage to take the Freedom March from any bondage that holds us captive, because bondage does not honor our Loving Father, no matter what period of time in our country's history—no matter what the American Moment.

FROM NUMBERS TO NELLY

by Mary J. Dixon Lebeau,
Woodbury, New Jersey

H er name was Nelly Adler. For a little while, it was my
name too.

Six million Jews, and millions of others, were exe-
cuted during the holocaust. They were beaten, tortured,
gassed—methodically murdered. For years, they were face-
less casualties, but recent efforts have put faces to those numbers, letting us personalize the loss—and learn from it.

At the United States Holocaust Memorial Museum in
Washington, D.C., as visitors check in at the door, they
receive an identification card, a passport into the past. That's
how I became Nelly Adler. I read the front of the card: "For
the dead and the living we must bear witness." I opened the
cover to gaze into long-ago eyes.

Nelly was born February 28, 1930, in Liege, Belgium. *So
she celebrated a birthday a day before mine,* I thought, feeling
vaguely connected to the dark-eyed girl in the oversized bon-
net. She was the youngest of three daughters born to Czecho-
slovakian parents, and her family was a Jewish family living in
a primarily Catholic town. Though her parents spoke Yiddish,
Nelly grew up speaking French like her friends.

As I traveled the exhibit floors, I learned more about
life for Nelly and her family during the Nazi regime. The
terror hit home first as synagogues and businesses were
razed, windows smashed, school doors shut. Then the Adlers
and other families were sent to ghettos, where everyone,
including twelve-year-old Nelly, was forced to work in

sewing factories or at hard labor.

According to my identification card, Nelly's father was in a hospital, seriously ill, when the family was awakened at 5 A.M. by the Gestapo's angry shouts.

"Where is your father?" they demanded.

"He's in the hospital," the sleepy girl answered.

"Liar!" one official yelled, slapping Nelly's face.

The household was arrested. They never saw Mr. Adler again.

I wandered through the rooms that depicted horrors of the concentration camps. I stood in the small, windowless wooden train car where Jews and others were packed together and transported to the camps. Although I knew I was safe, I began to understand the fear. I wondered how Nelly sustained her faith, knowing that prayer would be my only comfort on this train.

"We also exalt in our tribulations," I reminded myself, whispering the Bible verse. When these people deboarded the train, the Gestapo took their belongings. The Adlers weren't suspicious, since this had happened when they were forced into the ghetto. Then Mrs. Adler and her daughters were taken to a large showering area and were told to remove their clothing.

"You must be showered to kill the lice," they were told.

On the last page of the identification card in the Holocaust museum, you read of your fate. On that camp visit, everyone in my party was liberated.

Everyone except Nelly.

With her mother and sisters, she and others waited for the water to hit. But the water never came. Instead, the room filled with lethal gas. Nelly Adler died in Auschwitz on May 21, 1944, at fourteen years old.

The horror didn't stop there. After death, the bodies were brought here, where gold fillings were removed from their teeth and their hair was cut to sell for wigs. Then, ten at a time, the bodies were cremated.

As I left the area, feeling stunned at the fate I shared with Nelly, I completed the Bible verse I had whispered earlier, "We also exalt in our tribulations, knowing that tribulation brings about perseverance and perseverance, proven character and proven character, hope" (ROMANS 5:3–4 NASB). I know that hope will continue, even in the dark days. Even when we can't understand the horror, we must hope—and remember.

So I will remember not only the six million Jews and millions of others, but also the sixty thousand Vietnam casualties, the 296 deaths from Oklahoma City, and those thousands stolen from us in September 2001. All these moments in history have turned countless hearts toward God.

Most of all, I'll forever remember one little girl. Her name was Nelly Adler. For a little while, I shared her name.

BODY COUNT

by Rev. Michael F. Welmer,
Houston, Texas

For so many of my generation, the Vietnam War was the most significant event that affected our relating, thinking, and believing. For me, not the war, but the reporting of it, formed much of my future political, religious, and moral soil.

Nightly newscasts delivered war's horrors and gave a "body count." On the bottom of the television screen would flash the total number of dead, wounded, and missing in action. Every day the count climbed from hundreds to tens of thousands.

Over the years, the memory of daily body counts shaded my perception of the sanctity of life. It has instilled in me a deep appreciation for the value of every human life.

We can live for months far removed from the sting of death. But what if each day we faced a "body count"? What if the evening news provided a running total of how many died from drugs, drunk drivers, neglect and abuse, gang wars, and domestic violence? Would such a tally sensitize us to others' perils? Would it energize us to be more caring, accepting, and embracing?

Would a daily body count of those perishing without knowing Jesus Christ stir the hearts of God's people to greater passion for the lost?

The presence of a daily body count raised my consciousness. Years in the Lord's service have taught me that we are constantly engaged in a war that exists on many fronts. It is an engagement against the onslaught of the evil one and evil forces. The total body count from this war is staggering. Each of God's people needs to dedicate himself or herself to the mission of realizing that every body counts!

OUT OF THE WHIRLWIND

by Linda Tinker,
Oklahoma City, Oklahoma

What? Is everyone okay?" Candy turned her head away from her cell phone to fill us in. "An F5 tornado has hit back home!"

I, along with other coworkers, had traveled to North Carolina from Oklahoma City on our company's plane for a Special Olympics event. The rush of customers at our merchandise tent had dwindled as athletes and volunteers headed to the main event. Candy had taken advantage of the respite to call home on her cell phone.

One by one we used Candy's cell phone to call our families. After failing to reach my daughter, Deborah; my son, David; or my brother, Mike, I finally got through to my sister Patti.

"Patti! What's going on?" I shouted.

"I'm in the bathtub," she replied.

"You're taking a bath?" I asked.

"No," she shouted. "I'm lying in the bathtub with Rylee [her granddaughter]. We can hear the tornado coming. It sounds awful! I'm so scared!"

The phone went dead. I redialed her number, but the line was gone. After trying for several more hours to reach my family in Oklahoma, I called my sister Karen in Georgia.

"I'm so glad to hear your voice," Karen said. "We've been watching the tornado coverage. I've been trying to call you. Are you okay?"

"I'm in North Carolina, Karen," I explained. "I can't get

through to Oklahoma City and was hoping Patti might have called you."

"I haven't heard from her," Karen replied, "but CNN is showing the damage right now." She suddenly gasped. "Oh, no, that's Patti's subdivision. Nothing is left!"

The three-hour flight home that night seemed to take an eternity. We arrived at three o'clock in the morning, unexpectedly greeted by our CEO. Fear gripped me. Had he come to tell me my sister had been killed?

"Linda, your house has been hit, but your daughter and dogs are okay," he said. "We're to call your brother Mike so he can come get you."

"What about my sister?" I asked. He shook his head. "Maybe Mike knows something."

We couldn't get to my house because roads were blocked with debris and power lines were down. The city looked so eerie. Most of the homes and businesses were without electricity, and traffic lights weren't working. Deborah and I went to Mike's house, where we dozed fitfully.

Mike drove us to our neighborhood that morning. As I saw the devastation, I sobbed. Homes were rubble. Trees were stripped. The sea of green surrounding my home was gone. Cars were scattered—some stacked on top of each other.

I was relieved to see my home still standing. The garage door was buckled, and the gutter was hanging. But as we entered the front door, I cried again. The kitchen had collapsed. Papers, broken glass, and a mixture of dirt, oil, and heaven knows what else covered the walls and furniture. The wall between the living room and garage was buckled. Torn linen curtains flapped through broken windows. Part of someone else's roof was in my backyard. My doghouse and picnic table were gone. The gas grill was ruined. The trees, shrubs, and roses I had planted in honor of each grandchild's birth were gone.

I wept as I watched neighbors sift through debris. But even in those first moments, peace came over me with the assurance that all my circumstances were in God's hands. Nothing could touch me unless He permitted it. I felt sure He had a purpose in allowing this to happen.

We finally heard from Patti later that day. She and Rylee escaped without a scratch. Patti salvaged few belongings from the rubble that had been her home, but she did not despair. We both had put ourselves in the hands of a gracious, loving God.

Over the next few months, as we lived in temporary lodgings, we grieved at times. But we both were confident that God had everything under control. In truth, God had been dealing with me for some time about divesting myself of some of the things I was so attached to. This stripping process had already begun in some areas of my life. But I had been unwilling to let go of the house where I felt secure, or the job that paid a good salary even though I yearned to find work that would be more meaningful—that would make a difference in God's kingdom.

I also had always wanted to own an older home in an historic area, but never thought I could afford it. Now I bought a small Tudor-revival house. I used insurance money to pay off all my debts, and within eighteen months I resigned from my job and went to work for a church.

The tornado let me see how many wonderful, caring people are around me. Strangers helped in so many ways. Churches dropped off boxes of food and supplies. Friends helped clear the debris, move our belongings, and provide food. Another friend lent me her cell phone for weeks. One couple offered the second floor of their home to Deborah and me.

In the aftermath, I saw God's awesome provision. My daughter and our dogs were safe. My son and his family were safe. My sister and her granddaughter climbed out of her bathtub unscathed even though the tornado destroyed everything around them except one bathroom wall.

Out of the whirlwind, I learned much. God can and does bring good out of any situation. He is unfailingly faithful and shows His love in ways we never expect. Through difficulty, He enlarges our perspective and lets us see what is really important. And if He has to use a catastrophe to change our direction, He will. No matter how great the loss, our God can restore beyond our imagining, and He can turn what seems like an ending into a wonderful beginning.

TOUR OF DUTY

by Marilyn Morsch,
Palm Desert, California

B oom! Just as we heard the explosion, the building started
to shake. At home in California, we would have guessed
this to be a 4.3 earthquake. But we weren't in California,
we were in Washington, D.C., and I didn't think the area
was prone to earthquakes.

My husband and I were touring the Mid-Atlantic states
in our trailer. On September 11, we parked our trailer in
Maryland and hopped on a subway, the Metro, to take us to
the heart of D.C. for a Pentagon tour we'd scheduled.

We went through the heavy security, put our personal
belongings in a closet, and received a badge to wear. Then we
passed through the security doors into the hallowed halls of
the Pentagon. We were about one-third of the way through
our tour when the blast hit. Our tour guide yelled three
pieces of information: Follow me (our route); to the Metro
exit (our destination); on the run (and our procedure)!

I knew our salvation depended upon following our
guide's instructions. Because my husband has artificial hips
and cannot run, a second Army officer tour guide stayed
with us in the chaos as employees poured out of the offices
into the halls. We finally dashed through the security doors,
where I swooped up my fanny pack. We passed our tour
guide and gave him our ID badges—the only identification
we had during the experience, and the only proof that we
had made it out safely.

When we reached the south parking lot, we turned and

saw billowing black smoke. From a blaring car radio, we learned about the terrorist attacks. We were told to move away from the building because a fourth plane was heading toward Washington, D.C.

When the F-16 military planes roared overhead, we knew protection had arrived. We watched the military set up triage and organize their troops. The Medivac helicopter made only one trip with the injured before all planes were grounded.

Our next challenge was to return to our trailer in Maryland. We began the long walk to the other side of the Pentagon where we saw flames, smoke, and the gaping hole. We knew this kind of damage meant many injuries and deaths. We climbed a wall into Arlington Cemetery for the long, long trip to a working subway.

The Washington, D.C., of days earlier, with wall-to-wall people, was now a ghost town. The streets were occupied only by police, military, a man in a suit running, and two tourists—us. But at the Metro station, life bustled. For two weeks we had seen people in D.C. with their heads in newspapers, talking to no one. Now people were making U-Turns toward communication, everyone was talking about what happened.

Even though we had heard about the World Trade Center towers, nothing prepared us for seeing their collapse on TV. We had been to the top two weeks earlier. As we watched TV reports, we finally reached our family to let them know we were okay.

The next day, we began the long trip to the West Coast. We saw flags hanging and "God Bless America," "United We Stand," and "Pray for Our Leaders" written everywhere. American pride came out in full force.

Folks at home learned where we had been during the terrorists' attack and asked questions that made me reevaluate my life. God challenged me to make a U-Turn and meet my responsibility to spread the Good News of Jesus Christ. While I am not shy about my faith, I have never been one to preach either. Now I had a story to tell, but how would I do it? I decided to change my Christmas letter from family news to my experience. I decided to send it to the people on my mailing list, and to anyone who sent me any letter, card, solicitation, or bill. My letter told about the experience and what I had learned. I clearly explained the Gospel.

After I sent the Christmas letter, my message began to take on a life of its own. People asked for copies to send out. I was asked to share an expanded version with several groups. Tapes of my talk were requested. E-mails of the letter even went to Africa.

God has given me a new perspective on my salvation. I have moved out of my comfort zone. Every time I am before a microphone my heart races. I am not a public speaker, but I believe I survived this experience for an opportunity not to be wasted. I am to glorify my God and spread His message of salvation and grace. Jesus states in Matthew 10:32, "Whoever acknowledges me before men, I will also acknowledge him before my Father in heaven." What a wonderful promise.

Now is the time for all of us to evaluate who and what is important to us in this life and for all of eternity. Now is the time to make a U-Turn toward God.

COVERING CONCERN WITH PRAYER

by Karen Harper DeLoach,
Statesboro, Georgia

I sat in the shade of the Heartland Chapel and gazed at the clock on the Oklahoma City National Memorial across the road. It was set at 9:01, representing a moment of destruction that stopped time for 168 people on April 19, 1995.

It was the first time I had returned to my hometown since the Memorial was built, and since a tornado had destroyed my sisters' homes. I had flown in from Georgia for my niece's wedding, a happy time of celebration. But this day was set aside for a somber purpose. I was visiting sites of loss: my parents' graves, the empty lots where Linda's and Patti's houses had been, and now, the Memorial. As I sat in the beautiful little open-air chapel, I cried for the pain my family and other Oklahomans had suffered.

I had been working at my desk when I heard about the bombing of the Murrah Building. Distressing hours passed before I could reach my family. I finally learned all of our family was safe, although Linda's son had been trying to find a parking space on the opposite side of the building when the blast went off—he was running late for jury duty.

The next time tragedy struck, I was cooking supper when my husband hollered, "Karen, come here! CNN is showing tornadoes in Oklahoma! It looks bad!"

What I saw on TV truly frightened me. I had seen tornado devastation before, but not of this magnitude. We learned seventy-six tornadoes ripped through Oklahoma that day, with an F5 tornado staying on the ground for four hours, leaving a thirty-eight-mile path of destruction. I had seen my sister's flattened subdivision on CNN and spent an agonizing night before I learned that all my family was safe.

I used to let weeks, even months, go by without contacting my brother and sisters. No more. Life is too tenuous. It's too easy to lose those you love. Now when I say goodbye, I try to add an "I love you." It may be the last time I can tell them that.

It's hard living far away from my family. When they are going through tough times, it's even worse. I want to give them a hug, to see their expressions when they say, "I'm okay"—because no matter how hard things are, they always say, "I'm okay."

Before I left the Heartland Chapel that day, I prayed for those who had suffered losses. I said a prayer for my brother, my sisters, and their families. I can't always be with them, but I can cover them with prayer and entrust them to a loving heavenly Father. And, in the end, that's more than enough.

A MATTER OF PERSPECTIVE

by Carmen Leal,
Naples, Florida

I don't remember what we were arguing about on January 28, 1986, at 6:37:53.444 A.M. Hawaiian time, but I know my husband and I were again at odds. We'd had more bad times than good in eight years of marriage. In a counseling session my pastor asked what we fought about. I retorted that the real issue was, "What don't we fight about?" We agreed on nothing from finances to children to values. A new Christian, I knew arguing with my husband wouldn't please God or solve our problems. But that didn't stop me from quarreling with as much fervor as my non-believing spouse.

As we drove over the Pali Highway for our daily commute from Kailua to Honolulu, the radio was tuned to the news station. I heard only snatches of news stories as I focused on making my point—the right point, of course.

As we entered the tunnel, a special live report interrupted the normal program. But we lost transmission. We bickered so intently about what could be so important that when we emerged from the tunnel and the static cleared, we almost missed the announcement. The *Challenger* had exploded.

The beauty of the majestic emerald velvet Koolau Mountains and the brilliance of the aqua waters mocked my feelings of confusion and despair. My unhappiness with my husband, my marriage, and my life no longer mattered. An unspoken truce silenced us for the rest of the commute. We listened to the broadcast as we inched our way down Bishop Street before turning onto Kapiolani. My tears fell as I saw clusters of brightly dressed business people obviously discussing the news in front of office buildings and open spaces. I offered up a prayer for the astronauts and their families.

It was anything but business-as-usual that morning as employees and management crowded into the conference room to view televised images of a mission gone so horribly wrong. Murmurs of disbelief mingled with sobs set the tone, as we watched the two solid rocket boosters corkscrew across the sky, trailing brilliant white plumes of frozen vapor. In mounting horror we watched as the ship broke up and fell blazing into the sea.

Television monitors at the spaceport showed paramedics parachuting into the sea. A rescue force was dispatched to see what might be done. We watched the men unload the remains of the seven recovered from the Atlantic Ocean.

Eventually I went back to my office until it was time for the evening commute. As we inched through rush-hour traffic, my husband and I listened to updates about the *Challenger* and its six astronauts and one teacher. Ellison Onizuka, the first Japanese-American astronaut, was from Hawaii. Hawaii's newscasters repeatedly mentioned his name and birthplace.

A contemplative mood replaced the tense atmosphere of the morning ride. As we approached the nursery school to pick up our sons, I thought about Ellison's wife, Lorna, and their two children. Suddenly my marriage didn't seem so disastrous.

The children's laughter greeted me as I walked into Sunshine Preschool. My active, healthy sons ran to me, chattering. In comparison, two children in Hawaii that day would never again see their father. A wife would never get to make up after an argument. Spurred by thoughts of an intact family, and grateful that I could still work out our problems, I thanked God as I held each child by a hand and walked them to the car.

The state of my marriage that day had felt hopeless. My husband and I each needed to change things. Before that day, I had been trying to solve every problem instead of trusting God for guidance, comfort, and hope. Trusting God meant relinquishing the safe yet faulty methods I had devised to get through each day. Now I needed to act out my faith. That meant loving my husband as God had outlined in 1 Corinthians 13.

The *Challenger* wasn't a catalyst that healed my marriage, but it drew me closer to God and taught me to trust Him with my entire life. It also changed my perspective about what constitutes a disaster, and it precipitated a major U-Turn in my life. That day I realized that as long as I have faith, I have hope. And as long as there's hope, nothing is a disaster.

THE VOCABULARY LESSON

by Sandra McGarrity,
Chesapeake, Virginia

P resident Kennedy has been shot. He has been taken to the hospital." Our fifth-grade classroom gasped as our teacher, eyes brimming, made the announcement.

"Good! I hope the n—r-lover dies!" the girl sitting in front of me exclaimed.

Thirty children froze in horror as the words ricocheted around the classroom. It was as if our president had taken another bullet before our eyes. Mrs. Johnson tried to resume class, but I didn't take in a thing she said during the next hour or so.

I don't know which announcement was the most shocking. I couldn't believe someone—especially a child—would speak of the President like that. We had watched him on television from his campaign to his election and inauguration, to the news broadcast the night before. My sister had a scrapbook of newspaper clippings and photographs of President Kennedy and his family. We quoted his famous words, "Ask not what your country can do for you, ask what you can do for your country." He was our hero.

Since we lived in the heart of the South, of course we'd heard the vulgar word that student used. But I'd never heard it spoken so vilely. I wondered if there was some connection between that word and the reason someone gunned down my beloved president.

A few years earlier, I had noticed that the dark-skinned people she accused him of loving had to go to a little side window at the drive-in dairy bar. When I went to the movies, I saw them pay on the other side of the ticket booth before they went up the outside stairway to the balcony. I noticed the separate rest rooms marked "Colored." I feared that I would get sick if I drank from the "Colored" water fountain. Maybe because it was so rusty and dirty when the one marked "White Only" was shiny clean. I never understood. Was she saying that President Kennedy didn't understand it either?

Before long, someone announced that our President had died. Most of us burst into tears, including the girl. She buried her face in her arms and cried, "I didn't mean it." A few girls tried to comfort her, but no one could take back her ugly words.

I would like to say I never said unkind, angry words after that day, but that wouldn't be true. However, when I express angry words, the Lord often reminds me of that day in fifth grade, that "American Moment." As I remember, I realize how words can also fatally wound.

"Likewise the tongue is a small part of the body,
but it makes great boasts.
Consider what a great forest is set on fire by a small spark."
JAMES 3:5

THE DAY I BECAME A MAN

by Michael L. Anderson, Ball Ground, Georgia,
as told by Charles L. Anderson

Drizzle tapped on the windows that dreary December 7 Sunday in 1941. Our cozy little home in Munster, Indiana, hosted familiar aromas. Morning coffee brewed, my little sister burned toast, and starch from my mother's endless ironing wafted through the rooms. The big radio played softly. The radiators hissed. No church today. The roads were too bad. It would be a cold, lazy day, with only eighteen more until Christmas.

Papa was in the living room, beginning to read the heavy Chicago newspaper. I couldn't even think about touching most sections of it until he finished them. So I sat on the floor in my flannel pajamas, working on a project for social studies at Hammond High. I was thirteen.

To pass the time, I cut out articles about the war in Europe to support my views on isolationism. Mama said I was idealistic. "Charles, it's not a perfect world we live in, and we may someday have to help our friends over there."

The radio program was suddenly silenced as an announcer said, "Stand by for an important announcement from the President of the United States."

The static didn't keep us from hearing our President's voice. Japanese military airplanes had attacked Pearl Harbor. He called December 7, 1941, "a day that will live in infamy." I could hear myself swallow as I remembered to breathe again.

"Those dirty Japs," my father said.

The seed of anger toward this apparent adversary grew.

I was impressed by my parents' seriousness, but lacked the wisdom to know what it meant.

None of us knew where Pearl Harbor was located. Mom thought it was in Hawaii. I wasn't sure about Hawaii's whereabouts, but I knew it was in the Pacific Ocean and maybe near the Philippines. My father said it was a United States territory and that we also had troops in Guam and Wake Island and in the Pacific. My sister got the globe by the bookcase. We found Hawaii. My mother said we should pray. What was I to pray for? Where was God right now? Was He sleeping in on this Sunday morning?

I knew there'd been a war in Europe for some time now. The steel mill my father worked in sold scrap iron to Britain to make combat airplanes. We learned about Hitler in school. It seemed even the Italians were helping the Nazis' war efforts. And now the Japanese? Yet Europe seemed so far away. We were living comfortably in the United States with a big ocean on each side of us. And it was almost Christmas. We didn't need to think about war just now.

Papa turned off the radio and went to his workshop. His frustration lingered. My father was a proud American who always seemed disappointed that he had been too young to fight in World War I. Now Papa would probably be too old.

My mother decided my sister and she should make gingerbread. I dressed and climbed through the snowdrifts to my best friend's house. Harvey and I spent the afternoon wondering when we might be old enough to enlist in the Army and if our girlfriends would miss us. His parents were angry at the Japanese. "Well, that's it," they decided. "We're going to war now."

That night after my family had gone to bed, I tuned in to the news broadcasts reporting Pearl Harbor casualties.

The loss of life stunned me. I pressed my ear against the radio, and tears welled up in my eyes. "Please, God, help me understand why," I prayed.

Talk was tough among my classmates the next day. Anger reigned, directed at the Japanese. Even my social studies teacher said, "We need to pay them back."

I called my girlfriend, Evelyn, that night. We talked for an hour. She was the only one I knew who felt compassion toward the Japanese. I knew of only one oriental family. They operated a laundry on the north side of town. Their oldest daughter, Suzy, was in my homeroom. She didn't come to class that Monday. I never saw her again. I don't even think she was Japanese. Anger grew toward anyone with slanted eyes. Ironically, many of my friends had German heritage, and no one seemed upset over them.

Everyone realized the United States was going to war. The isolationists became silent. Those who disliked President Roosevelt now supported him. The world was changing, and like it or not, I was changing too. God was beginning a U-Turn in me.

The following Sunday our church was packed with people I'd never seen—searchers hoping to find God's direction. The choir sang Christmas carols. I listened to every word. I felt I was no longer just a teenager living in a country about to go into war. I was becoming a spiritual man of God. I was beginning a new journey and putting aside my childish ways.

That Sunday in December was a benchmark of my youth. It was a season of conflict and contrast—an American Moment that forced many to grow up. While our nation was preparing to go to war, I was surrendering to God and allowing Him to direct my steps. I became a man that year, and life would never again be the same.

GOD
ALLOWS
U-TURNS

NEW DIRECTION
U-TURNS

Therefore, if anyone is in Christ, he is a new creation;
the old has gone, the new has come!
2 CORINTHIANS 5:17

THE CROSSING

by Gary W. Plourde Sr.,
Sinking Spring, Pennsylvania

I was only eighteen years old, but armed to kill. In Vietnam, I strutted around in full combat gear—jungle boots; camouflage; utility belt; canteen; grenade pouch; bayonet or K-bar (a large grooved killing knife); flak-jacket; double bandoleers with several fully loaded M-16 clips; five to six more clips on my belt; and a helmet on my head.

As I sucked on a cigarette, I stalked the jungle looking for life to terminate. I didn't care that I was dirty and grubby. "Kill or be killed" was everyone's motto. On my helmet I had written, "My Country Right or Wrong But Still My Country," and I determined to do whatever it took to get home. I killed whomever I had to. . .whenever I had to. . .with whatever. And at the time, I didn't think much about God.

Death was common in Vietnam. People, friends, and enemies came and went like flies. Soldiers avoided tight friendships because the closer they became to someone, the more they grieved if that person was killed. Sometimes for a break from the war, I went into the village for a haircut. While I sat in the barber's chair, I talked with villagers. Sometimes at night after a patrol, ambush, or killings, I pulled the same villagers—even the barber—out of the barbed wire. I didn't know whom to trust.

One of my duties was to wrap the dead in body bags. I stacked them, like logs, on a cold cement morgue floor. As I prepared the dead to go home, I shooed flies from wounds bigger than my fists. I still see their faces under translucent plastic—warped images that stared straight ahead. Weary with fear about my own death, I began to pray that God would give me rest from the horror.

Then one dark night, halfway through my tour of duty, I met God, the Redeemer of eternal life. It was June 11, 1968, outside Khe Sahn, Vietnam. My outfit was exhausted and set in a perimeter for the night. We figured we'd be hit that night. I pleaded for my life with the Lord—although I didn't know Him as such then. But the God of second chances, the God who uses the bad to make things good, listened.

About 2 or 3 A.M., the North Vietnamese Army (NVA) attacked. Bullets zipped above our heads. Charred and mangled flesh surrounded us. Artillery and human beings screamed and exploded. After twenty minutes, the NVA penetrated our lines. I was ordered into hand-to-hand combat. Men screamed, cursed, and cried. A grenade hit my left knee and dropped on my foot. Get down, I told myself.

As I fell at about a forty-five-degree angle to the ground, it flashed in my face. I never heard the explosion. I was thrown spread-eagle about twenty-five feet through the air. I hit the ground seriously wounded and covered in blood. Shrapnel ripped holes in my body, smoke wafted up with the smell of iron and burnt flesh. My left leg was torn off at the knee. My blood soaked the earth around me. The pain drove me nearly insane, nerve endings scraping against each other, until, thankfully, I lost consciousness.

Somewhere in my unconsciousness, I saw myself under a blood-soaked sheet on a hospital gurney with doctors, nurses, and people in white moving around me. I suddenly understood.

God was everywhere—down on that bloody table and in the peaceful space where I hovered. He was in the jungles of

Vietnam and on the quiet streets of a small town. I had moved beyond emotions. My faith was beginning. I knew, for sure, that there is eternal life. I understood that unless a person has faith, he or she is hopeless.

I knew my time on God's earth was not over. I understood that even though I'd be handicapped, Jesus would be sufficient. My body would do what it needed. I was peaceful. I had made a U-Turn toward a better understanding of God's all-encompassing nature.

When I woke, a nurse and doctor stood next to the gurney. Blood and plasma ran intravenously into my body through my hand and neck. I was confused. I was unable to talk, but I rolled my head and looked at them.

"Son," the nurse said, "someone upstairs was looking out for you, because with these wounds and the blood you lost, you should be dead."

The doctor nodded. I wondered how many times he had seen my kind of death. I rolled my head back toward the ceiling, closed my eyes, and prayed.

"God. . .Jesus. . .I know You're there. Thank You for my life."

Vietnam was an American Moment that changed my life. Sometimes I remember the horror. I didn't like it there, but in Vietnam, I met the Lord. He became real to me. There, through my near-death U-Turn, God assured me that Jesus is always with me. Not just here on earth, but also in heaven, when at last I am face to face with Him again.

BATTLEFIELD PROMISES THAT LAST

by Dr. Don J. Hanson,
Santa Ana, California

D elivering documents in Okinawa seemed too tame. I wanted to do more than that. So I volunteered for service in Korea.

I'd joined the army on my seventeenth birthday—in time for the Korean War. I didn't know much about war. I knew even less about Korea. But I was seized by a desire to help my country and to bring freedom to that faraway land. So while my friends avoided the service, I proudly volunteered.

When I arrived in Korea, I was in more action than I knew existed. Mortar fire screamed overhead as our First Cavalry tried to go through a rough mountain pass. It seemed impossible that any of us would make it. In the middle of that fierce battle, I talked to God as I never had before. I had come to Christ when I was thirteen. I loved studying His Word; in fact, a buddy and I spent hours in Okinawa studying Navigators' Bible memory courses. But I was an "armchair" Christian—glad to know God, but not concerned about anyone else knowing Him. I was more interested in sports and plans to make lots of money when I became a civilian again.

But now on the front lines, I saw how quickly life could be snuffed out. I vowed to God that if He brought me out of this, I would spend my life in ministry—serving Him as wholeheartedly as I served my country—to help others find the joy I had found in Him.

Suddenly a mortar landed beside my buddy. The explosion killed him instantly. I fell, bleeding profusely from the shrapnel and not knowing if the medics would reach me.

Thankfully, they did. But I was so badly wounded I had to spend the next three years in hospitals. And I'm still so full of shrapnel I set off airport metal detectors. But I never turned back on my promise. Whenever I could, I'd witness to fellow GIs at the local "Victory Center." And the day I received my discharge I went to a Christian college to prepare for the ministry.

Over the years, I've worked in evangelism and pastorates from Illinois to Australia. I faced a massive heart attack ten years ago, but I'm still active in a local church.

Most people I've met over the years have considered battlefield promises as "fire insurance" and vows that are soon left behind. But just as my body is still filled with shrapnel from that long-ago battlefield, my soul is still filled with the joy of my Lord. I made a U-Turn that day and have never looked back. He has always kept all His promises to me. How thankful I am that the Lord helped me keep my battlefield promise to Him!

SURROUNDED BY THE ENEMY

by Tammera Ayers, St. Mary's, Ohio,
as told by Richard Spicer

W hy haven't I gotten my papers?" I asked the draft officer. I had just graduated from high school and knew if I got to Europe, I could win this world war for America.

"Go back home, son. You'll hear from us," he said.

I didn't wait long. Soon I was on Omaha Beach, a private in General Patton's Third Army, helping push the Germans out of France.

Soon after I arrived, we received new M-1 rifles. We stacked these every evening at suppertime. One evening, I picked up the last rifle. Strange, this was not my gun. It wasn't new. I shrugged it off.

The next morning, rain pelted down as our company crossed a river into battle. I carried a bazooka, while another officer hauled the rockets. We were under fire as soon as the raft hit shore. Throughout the day we flushed the Germans out of pillboxes, dug foxholes, and pushed the enemy back. But as we prepared to stand our ground, we learned of a counter attack. We were ordered to retreat.

Slowed by the weight of the bazooka, I tried to climb a wet slope and fell behind. But the Germans behind me weren't slowed down. Unable to reach my company, I climbed into a foxhole. But the bazooka was useless without rockets. My only defense against the three Germans was my rifle and one hand grenade.

I aimed the rifle, but a water bubble stuck in the peephole. I blew out the bubble, then fired the gun. Click. Nothing happened. I frantically fired again. Nothing. The gun was jammed.

I yanked out the clip. My hands shook as I fit a single shell in the barrel. I lifted the gun. It fired, and I shot one man. I fed the gun another bullet and hit a second man, but I was too slow—the Germans were closing in. Yanking the grenade out of my shirt, I pulled the pin, but I was too late. A German soldier held his gun against my head and ordered me to toss the grenade. I joined the German soldiers and a captured American medic.

A young German boy lay wounded on a makeshift stretcher. A soldier pointed at the boy, the medic, and me. Then he pointed to another German company across a field ablaze with American artillery fire. I knew we couldn't make it across that field carrying their wounded soldier. I was sick knowing my own men would shoot me down.

Grabbing one end of the stretcher, I yelled to the medic, "We'll run to the edge of the field, hit the ground, and I'll pray the Twenty-third Psalm. Then we'll run for it."

We ran, hunkered down at the edge of the field, and I fervently prayed, "The Lord is my shepherd, I shall lack nothing. . . . Even though I walk through the valley of the shadow of death, I will fear no evil, for you are with me. . . ."

We got up, ran across the field, climbed a fence, and arrived panting to a company of German soldiers. I don't know what that German boy said, but I think he told them not to hurt us. They ordered me into a sedan and took me to a small French village, leaving me with American POWs. Then, a German officer took me to another village. We stepped into a huge barn with German soldiers everywhere. I suspected they were waiting for orders of a counter attack.

I fell into a pile of hay. A German soldier approached, and I thought he would order me up, but he tossed a blanket over me. I slept through the night. In the morning, they brought in jam and sourdough bread. One of the men threw me a pocketknife and motioned towards the jam. "Put that on your bread and eat it," he said.

After we ate, I fell asleep again. When I awoke, someone had thrown an overcoat over me. Soon, they put me in a cattle stall.

"They're gonna search you," one soldier said. "If you let me hold your valuables, I'll make sure you get them back."

I didn't believe him. But feeling I had no choice, I handed him my gold class ring and the watch my brother had given me. The soldier soon returned and said they wouldn't search me after all. He handed back my watch and ring.

From there, I was held prisoner at Moosberg, Stalag VII A, about thirty-five kilometers northeast of Munich, Germany, with Ground Force enlisted men and Air Force officer evacuees from several allied nations. I was glad to be with Americans again.

I'd spent much of my childhood in church, and I knew God was real. So, when I faced the enemy, I knew my only option was to call on Him. I didn't deserve His intervention; I hadn't been living for Him. But when I prayed the Twenty-third Psalm, God heard. He guided me safely through the enemy's camp. The Bible says in Psalm 91:14–15, " 'Because he loves me,' says the Lord, 'I will rescue him; I will protect him, for he acknowledges my name. He will call upon me, and I will answer him; I will be with him in trouble, I will deliver him and honor him.' "

On April 29, 1945, at 10:30 P.M., tanks from the American fourteenth Armored Division crashed through double ten-foot barbed wire fences to liberate 110,000 Allied prisoners, including thirty thousand Americans. We were going home because men who risked their lives overpowered the enemy.

But I also knew I was going home because of God's grace.

FROM COLUMBINE TO COMFORT

by Stephanie Plank,
Littleton, Colorado

When my free hour rolled around at school, I headed for the library to study for a test. But then I ran into two friends who asked if I would like to have lunch at the mall instead. We left the school at 10:15 A.M., an hour before my life, and our school, Columbine, and even the town of Littleton would be turned upside down.

As we returned to school, we saw kids running across the street, looking scared. I figured the school must be having a fire drill. We had a few minutes before class, so we drove around the block and headed back to the school.

Out of nowhere a teacher stopped us in the middle of the street. "Go home!" he commanded.

"Why?" we asked.

"Just go home!" was all he could say.

Jokingly I asked, "What—is someone dead?"

"We hope not," the teacher replied.

My friends and I froze. Fear filled my heart. We raced to my friend's house and turned on the news. We all know how that story ends, but for me it was just the beginning.

The whole town of Littleton was seeking God, and I was too.

I was raised to know God existed, but I didn't know what being a Christian really meant. After my parents divorced, I'd gotten teased a lot. I would walk home from elementary school, and later tenth grade, and kids would throw rocks at me. Sticks and stones may break the bones, but words kill the spirit. When my family moved to Colorado, I decided I would never again be nerdy. I decided I would do whatever it took to fit in.

I found a group to hang out with and clung to the guys in the group. I started smoking pot and my life went downhill. The guys used me, and my heart grew cold from the pain. I started sneaking out at night, only to be brought home by the police. I watched my mother cry, but continued to get deeper into the trash. I was out of control. After the shooting, my heart cried for something more. I found a Christian youth organization called Young Life. That summer, kids in the group were going to a place called Frontier Ranch. I could feel something pulling me to go.

Along with my clothes, I took my anger, hurt, and bitterness. At Frontier Ranch I began to see that I was covered in sin. I thought Christ had been with me all my life, but because of my sin, I was really separated from Him. The people at the camp told me that through the blood of Jesus Christ and what He had done on the cross, I could be saved and washed clean. My heart was broken, and I fell to my knees. Jesus came into my heart. Out went the evil things that had dragged me down. My heart filled with happiness, relief, and joy. For the first time, I felt peace.

On July 24 I stepped off the bus a new person. My life began to change. My old friends invited me to the next party. With God's strength I walked away. I tried to share my faith with my old friends, but they left me.

The tragedy brought deep pain, but it also led to comfort. Through the lives of those who died, countless more were saved. I can't wait until I see the Christians who were martyred to thank them and show them they did not die in vain. So many bad things happen in the world, but God can turn pain into something beautiful. Thank You, God, for allowing U-Turns!

FAITH IN GEOMETRY CLASS

by Charles Gibson,
Centerville, Minnesota

t blew up! The *Challenger* blew up!"

I was in my high school library when the librarian shouted her announcement. I had been engrossed in a geometry assignment. I liked geometry because it made sense to me. I could apply theorems and corollaries to arrive at a final answer—definite proof. Proof that the world made sense, that I could bring order to my existence.

But at the librarian's announcement, my concentration was gone. Everything stopped. In the past such news might have filled me with anxiety, causing me to retreat into my own, safe, go-it-alone world. In those years, I hated any attention. I felt like people were too demanding, always wanting me to talk. Usually I wanted to learn about geography, history, or geometry rather than talk to my peers about frivolous things. Small talk was not my forte. People all described me the same: "You're quiet, aren't you?" I felt sentenced to solitary confinement.

Sometimes I would argue with them, sometimes I became extremely outgoing, other times I said nothing but thought, "My life is none of your business." But I was stubbornly quiet. Often when my parents wanted to know something, I would refuse to tell them. I controlled the flow of information about my life the way an anorexic controls food intake.

On January 28, 1986, when the *Challenger* exploded, I was a new Christian. I knew where I would go when I died, that I would spend eternity with God. But I wasn't sure about much else. As a small group of us in the library huddled around a television, a few girls cried and hugged each other. The news anchors tried to make sense of the freak accident as we watched replays. The *Challenger*, pushed by thousands of pounds of thrust, exploded as it was soaring toward triumph.

Many of my illusions about security in life were shattered in an instant. If one of the most sophisticated machines ever built could erupt into a ball of fire and smoke, then what about my weak attempts to figure out this life? What guarantees exist short of heaven?

It was a shock I had never felt before. I couldn't rid myself of the contrast: the *Challenger* breaking free of the earth's gravity, of the grip of this world, only to shatter and return to earth, dust to dust. Though shaken, I didn't feel hopeless. In spite of the depth of my emotions, God had hold of my life.

I stayed in the library until the bell rang. Then I headed for my geometry class. When I entered the room, most people knew something had happened to the *Challenger*, but didn't know what. Instead of taking my seat and feigning ignorance, I told whoever would listen that I had seen the space shuttle explosion on television.

"It blew up shortly after liftoff," I said. I had everyone's full attention. If I'd thought about my audience, I might have fumbled for words. The teacher nodded his head as if to encourage me.

"They think everyone was killed," I continued. "No one could have survived that explosion. There was no time for anyone to bail out." I shrugged my shoulders, adding, "I've never seen anything like it."

"Did that teacher die too, Chrissy-what's-her-name?" someone asked me.

"I think so," I said, looking at our geometry teacher. "She must have."

I sat down and began to tremble. My face itched, and I realized my cheeks were wet. I hadn't even noticed the tears. I said a silent prayer for our class and one for the families who had lost someone in the explosion, especially the family of Christa McAuliffe. It was the first time I had ever prayed for anyone without being asked.

From that point, I started to move toward people rather than away from them, trusting God for the strength to live this life. God started to show me how much people matter to Him, how much I matter to Him. I wanted other people to know the same thing. I continued to pray for the people in my geometry class and formed several friendships. I even had the opportunity to tell a few students about my faith in Christ.

Paul wrote in Romans 8:26, "The Spirit helps us in our weakness. We do not know what we ought to pray for, but the Spirit himself intercedes for us with groans that words cannot express." I knew God was present that day and that He helped me move beyond my anxiety to everyday faith in Him.

MR. J.

by Kathryn K. Howard,
Rochester, New York

D on't worry about Mr. J. Just tell him what you're doing, then go on to someone else," the Manhattan nursing home administrator told me, pointing to a gentleman in the corner alone.

"Why can't I give him a letter?" I asked.

"Well, he's blind, so why waste it?" she said.

"But these pictures are made of construction paper pasted onto more construction paper. They have texture. Can't I give him one and tell him what he's feeling with his fingers?" I was determined not to exclude anyone.

The administrator sighed. "Go ahead, but he won't talk to you. He hasn't talked to anyone since September 11."

I walked to Mr. J. and sat down beside him. "Mr. J., I'm Kathryn. I want to give you a picture that was made by a preschooler near Rochester. The kids there have been visiting people like you. They feel like the residents are extra grandmas and grandpas," I explained. "When they found out about what happened on September 11, they were worried about grandmas and grandpas here in the city and wanted to do something. They want you to know they are thinking about you and you're in their prayers."

Mr. J. was silent. I took his hand and moved it to the paper in front of him.

"This is a picture of a flower in a flowerpot." I moved his fingers over the flower petals. "The flower is bright purple." His fingers went to the stem. "The stem is green." He moved down to the flowerpot. "The flowerpot is orange. And there is a bright blue sky and a golden yellow sun shining down on the flower." Mr. J.'s hand stopped moving.

"This picture was made by Davy and he's four. He wrote a message on the back of the picture. It says, 'I am hoping for you.' "

Mr. J.'s face crumpled. His sightless eyes filled with tears. He hoarsely whispered, "I felt it."

I didn't quite understand. "I'm sorry, Mr. J., you felt what?"

"When they fell. I felt them fall," he explained softly.

"Oh, Mr. J., I am so sorry." My tears mixed with his as we cried for the lost souls and hopes and dreams that died on that awful day. Then we talked about being scared and not knowing what to do. He told me about sitting in the TV room, hearing about the plane crashes, and finally, the fall of the Towers.

"I knew before they said it on the TV," Mr. J. remarked. "I felt the vibrations through the floor. I didn't know what it was. I never felt anything like it before. I was so scared. How could someone do that to us? Why?"

I had no answer. We sat for awhile longer holding hands. Then it was time to go. I hugged him. "Please take care of yourself, Mr. J."

He smiled and patted my hand. "I'll be fine now, girl, don't you worry. And you give that Davy a big 'thank you' for me. Wait a minute. I'll do it myself. I'll Braille that boy a note and tell him myself. Can I do that? Can you get a letter back to him?"

I laughed. "You bet I can. And won't you make him happy! You write that note, and I'll come back and get it from you."

Mr. J. was silent and I got up. He leaned forward suddenly and spoke again.

"Maybe this is the good that can come out of the evil. Maybe just having folks reach out to one another is the message we're supposed to get. They can bend us, but they will never break us. I'll tell Davy that in my note."

"You do that, Mr. J. And I'll make sure that everyone else gets the message too."

I gathered up my things to leave. The administrator took me aside.

"What on earth did you do to Mr. J.?" she quizzed. "This is the first time he's said anything more than yes or no since September 11. What did you say to him?"

I shrugged my shoulders. "It wasn't me, it was the message Davy sent that helped him to speak. I was just here to make sure Mr. J. got the letter."

"Then God bless Davy," she said as she smiled at me.

I smiled back. "Amen."

ONE LOST SHEEP

by Elizabeth Griffin,
Edmonds, Washington

W hen Curt Adams answered a call to join an outreach team in New York City, he had no idea that God was calling him to be His shepherd.

Early one morning, a week after the World Trade Center buildings collapsed, Curt and three other men from his church in Mt. Vernon, Washington, climbed into a van and headed east. After forty-nine hours, they joined others in New Jersey and went to Union Square in New York City. Their mission was to minister Christ's comfort to the thousands at a twenty-four-hour candlelight memorial service.

With the stench of burning buildings stinging their nostrils, teams of Christians were listening to, praying for, and wiping away the tears of a mourning crowd. Putting away well-worn methods of street evangelism, they came as Christ's body to support and heal.

As one woman began to share the story of Nicodemus with another, Curt noticed a man listening. Just as Nicodemus had approached Jesus in secrecy, this man was edging closer. Curt then began to talk to the man. Omar, a Middle Eastern man who followed the religion of Islam, told Curt, "There are times that I want to know Jesus, and times that I don't."

Curt explained the gospel, emphasizing the grace God has for each of us. When Curt said, "God wants you to make a U-Turn in your life and leave your sin behind to follow Him," Omar quickly responded, "Yes, that's what I want!" They prayed and one lost lamb was brought into the Lord's fold for all eternity.

The Lord had called a man to drive all the way from Washington State to New York City just to find one lost sheep. That's how much He loves us.

FAITH UNDER FIRE

by Angel Brown,
Westbury, New York

O n October 28, 2001, the walls shook and the windows
shimmied as two explosions, a minute apart, rocked my
neighborhood. I'd been coping fairly well with the terrorist attacks until then. Ground Zero was several miles
away. Except for the unmistakable stench of destruction riding on the shifting wind, I maintained my sanity by limiting
my intake of news.

That October evening, however, I watched our
President's televised address to the nation. His defiant,
upbeat attitude was reassuring, but his warning of further
threats struck fear in my heart. I turned off the TV to get my
nine-year-old daughter, Shannon, ready for bed. I knew
when she asked me to sleep with her that night that his
words had frightened her.

"You don't need to be scared, sweetheart," I tried to reas-
sure her. "Our government's doing a good job of protecting
us. That's what they're here for."

Two hours later, I stood petrified as the first blast roared
through the neighborhood. I ran to Shannon's room, where
I found her sleeping, oblivious to the sirens and shouts. I
cracked the front door open. I spotted my landlord, who
lives just down from my apartment.

"What was that?" I croaked.

"Sounded like an explosion," he gruffly answered. As he
snapped open the deadbolt on the building's outer door, the
second blast assaulted the night air. The landlord's wife and

eleven-year-old son appeared in their doorway.

"Call 911," squeaked the boy.

"I'm going out to see what's going on," his father barked. "Lock the door behind me."

"Don't!" we chorused, but he stepped out and shut the door firmly.

"Any idea what's going on?" I asked.

"We heard that a manhole cover blew off and a car blew up about two blocks away. Then another manhole cover blew off ten blocks away."

I stared at her. She shrugged. We didn't want to speculate in front of her son, but I could see the question in her eyes: Was our sleepy neighborhood under attack? Thankfully, we were spared further explosions. After the wail of sirens died, I crept into Shannon's bed.

Like most New Yorkers, after the September 11 attacks, I'd dug in my heels against the overwhelming urge to flee. When Mayor Giuliani and President Bush urged us to remain calm, to continue our normal lives, I tried to comply. I proudly hung the stars and stripes in my front window, and I went about my business as if I weren't afraid.

But exploding manhole covers were too much for me to handle. After dropping Shannon off at school the next morning, I called my sister, Maureen, in Colorado.

"Maybe it's time for you to move," she rationalized, as I sobbed. "You know we'd love to have you. Dad and Alex would be thrilled." She and her fourteen-year-old daughter, Alex, lived only a few miles from our dad.

I'd thought about moving closer to my family, but I loved New York. I'd lived there for fifteen years, with occasional forays to other states and cities. But I always returned to the city that had stolen my heart. Besides, I was now a middle-aged parent with a school-aged child. I couldn't keep living the nomadic lifestyle.

"I just don't know if I'm ready to leave," I cried. Fear, resentment, and anger broiled inside me. I hated being forced to consider a decision I was not ready to make by unknown entities who had no right to control my life.

"I guess my reasons for staying have changed," I mused. "It would probably be better for Shannon if we lived near you." My lack of conviction echoed in my ears. Whatever spell New York had over me hadn't been broken by the terror. "I'll keep you posted," I promised.

Later that night, as I told a good friend, "I don't want to leave New York, but I don't think it's safe to stay either. What am I going to do?" Tears pricked the back of my eyes. Then, a thought drifted into my consciousness. "Be patient. I'll give you the answer."

Instantly, my burden swept away in a flood of relief and serenity. God had heard my plea. I'd been letting my faith dwindle, but now, with vivid clarity, I realized my faith had made a U-Turn. God was with me, and always had been. He would see me through this crisis.

I'm still in New York, still standing in the face of my fears, but now I feel safe because I know God is standing beside me.

THE WAKEUP CALL

by Carlin Randall Hertz,
Waldorf, Maryland

I was running on the treadmill at the gym when I started to watch NBC Today on the TV overhead. Suddenly, the program was interrupted. One of the World Trade Center towers was ablaze. Even the news anchor didn't know what had happened. I watched in horror as another plane flew into the second Twin Tower. I raced to the locker room to shower.

Hundreds of federal government workers stared like zombies at their TVs when I arrived at the office. I looked out the window and saw black smoke filling the air. On the TV, the anchor reported that the Pentagon had burst into flames. It was fifteen miles from my office.

I tried to call my pregnant wife, but the phones were dead. I started to panic. That's only fifteen miles away. *Could this be the end of my life?* I wondered. Rodger, a coworker who was leaving, asked if I wanted to hitch a ride.

"Yes," I said. I grabbed my belongings, and Rodger, David, and I headed for the elevators. Outside, the nation's capital was in total disarray. People were screaming and running to their cars. Traffic was backed up for miles.

In my coworker's truck, I silently prayed, "Lord, just let me get home to my family. If this is it, let me die with them." After going only a mile in thirty minutes, David and I decided we'd fare better on foot. Union Station was a block away, but when we got there, it was shut down.

"Eastern Market is about fifteen blocks away. Want to

take that hike?" David asked.

I was determined to get out of the city. We tried short-cuts to the subway station but were stopped each time. "These streets are closed. Go another way," yelled a police officer. Finally we made it to the open subway station, which was packed with nervous people. When I got home three hours later, I hugged my wife and son, and rubbed my unborn child. "I love you. Baby, you just don't know how happy I am to see you all," I said as I hugged my family again. I thanked God for getting me back in their arms.

That day reopened my eyes to the Lord. I started walking with Him faithfully again. I learned that God was tired of our misplaced priorities. America was founded on godly principles many of us had forgotten or shunned.

God used the tragedy to save thousands of lost souls, encouraging U-Turns toward Him in record numbers. If the terrorist events hadn't happened, my Christian walk would probably still be like running on the treadmill—running hard but getting nowhere fast.

I thank God I didn't die that morning. I thank God that He gave me another chance to get my life in order. Thank You, Jesus.

FOUNDATION OF FAITH

by Marie Jones,
San Marcos, California

I had finally finished reading my book and fallen asleep around 2:40 A.M. The next thing I knew I was shaken awake. As I opened my eyes to a pitch-black room, I immediately knew what was happening. An earthquake. A big one.

My husband and I had lived through many Los Angeles earthquakes, but the January 17, 1994, Northridge quake was different. The bed shook so hard we had to hang on to keep from being hurtled against the walls. We called out to God and said good-bye to each other as the floors beneath us groaned and lurched. Every sound was frightening: breaking glass, fire alarms, car alarms, and shattering wood. Our second-story Burbank apartment swayed and jerked for what seemed like an eternity. When the shaking stopped, we were frozen in fear. Just when we got the courage to take action, the first aftershock hit. It was almost as big as the quake itself.

Finally, we ran out the door, down two flights of stairs, and joined our neighbors in the cold winter air. The quake claimed nearly sixty lives and seriously injured another fifteen hundred. The damage totaled billions of dollars. Recovery would take a long time.

But the real recovery for my husband and me occurred later. The earthquake had jolted our foundation in more ways than one. We began to wonder if pursuing our dreams of working in Los Angeles's entertainment industry was what we really wanted. We missed our families. It seemed like we only worked to afford living in costly L.A.

Suddenly, the glitter of the City of Angels had lost its appeal. We yearned for peace, quiet, and a place where we could put down roots near our family. But did we have the faith to leave the high life behind? Could we make a U-Turn? Our foundation of faith was tested. We prayed.

Within six months, we quit our jobs and moved to San Diego, where we later bought a home and had a child. We started a multimedia production company. And we praise God, who used the Northridge earthquake to put us in a new, wonderful life. All we had to do was open ourselves to His guidance and follow His lead.

TERROR IN THE NIGHT

by Bonnie M. Alba,
Hanford, California

had just put the children to bed on a stormy evening, April 3, 1974. Friends arrived for our weekend canasta game. Focused on our game, we barely noted the TV weatherman announcing possible tornadoes. Then we heard, "There's a tornado on the ground in southwestern Alabama headed northeast into Tennessee." Sirens blared, and he continued giving warnings for areas west and north of us. Game forgotten, we watched as the weatherman pointed to green tornado blips on the radar.

We still felt safe in our army housing on Redstone Arsenal. A range of hills separated us from the tornadoes. But our uneasiness increased as the weatherman reported tornadoes slamming into trailer parks and cutting swaths across small towns. He reported deaths and injuries in other states.

None of us had ever been in a tornado. We decided to follow the weatherman's safety tips. Just in case. We filled plastic jugs with water and slightly opened some windows so the house wouldn't explode.

The wind intensified and blew the heavy rain horizontally. We couldn't see the houses across the street. One gigantic lightning flash lit up the sky before the electricity went off. Stumbling in the dark, we found flashlights and lit candles.

Our husbands kept going outside to catch the latest weather updates on the car radio. Dozens of tornado sightings were reported in our area. Sirens wailed outside our home. Over the roar of the storm, a booming voice shouted through the loud speaker, "Take shelter now! In the center area of your quarters! Use mattresses to protect yourselves in hallways!"

Our bathroom was in the center of our house. We quickly roused our children from their beds and rushed them into the bathtub with blankets and pillows. Then we waited. Curious, we crawled to look out the front windows.

Thirty minutes passed, when the wind died down and the rain stopped. It was calm and pitch black. Suddenly a high-pitched whistle pierced the air. As we peered toward the hills, the blackness became ghostly green. Our husbands yelled, "Run for the bathroom!" All of us, four adults and three children, crammed into a bathroom barely big enough for two.

The whistle deepened, like the sound of a roaring train. We held our hands over our ears and felt as if our bodies were vibrating. It was over our heads and inside with us. That's when I prayed to the God I had ignored for years. I pleaded with Him for our children's lives, if not my husband's or mine.

In terror, we clung to each other. Our children cried. Time stopped. We lived a lifetime in that tiny, suffocating dark room. Finally we noticed the sound diminishing. My husband snapped on the flashlight. In the dim light, our faces mirrored fear and hope. Could the tornado have turned away from us?

It had, this twister that was part of the worst tornado outbreak in U.S. history. One hundred forty-eight tornadoes touched down within sixteen hours. In their twenty-five-hundred-mile trail they left 330 dead and 5484 injured.

In Alabama, 86 people died, with 949 injured. Damages exceeded fifty million dollars. After a long, terrifying night, we thankfully emerged into the morning sun. We had survived. We kept hugging our children and each other.

Later we saw what this F3 tornado did. It hit the barracks, tossed cars into jumbled piles, jumped over the guard hut and main road, spared three houses, and demolished a small church.

I have no doubt now that those life-threatening moments in one of the darkest nights of my life were God's wakeup call to me. God planted a seed in my heart. Fifteen years would pass, with many starts and stops, before I finally fully surrendered to Him. But I'm thankful the twist of a tornado brought a U-Turn in my life, to begin me back on the right path.

GOD
ALLOWS
U-TURNS®

FAMILY
STRENGTH

The Lord is my light and my salvation—
whom shall I fear?
The Lord is the stronghold of my life—
of whom shall I be afraid?

PSALM 27:1

FINDING FAITH

by Ann Coogler,
Salem, South Carolina

The drums rolled a solemn cadence from the television. The body of our President lay on the caisson. Shock hung in the air of my aunt's house. Our close-knit family changed from our own funeral attire and gathered to watch. Death wrapped its icy claws around my family and an entire nation at the same time.

A few days earlier, my mother and I had talked over breakfast. "Your hairdo makes you look so grown-up," Mama remarked on my attempt to emulate Jackie Kennedy's fashionable appearance.

"You are picking me up so that I can have my hair done at the beauty parlor?"

My question was more like a demand.

"Yes, I'll be there," Mama responded.

My ashen-faced father picked me up from school in the early afternoon. As I sat in the car, his sobbing words came slowly.

"It's your mother. She's gone."

My heart raced wildly. "What do you mean?"

"She's dead. I found her; they think it was a cerebral hemorrhage."

The mother with whom I shared so many things—a love of reading, long talks, beach trips, shopping, laughter, and tears—was dead. Her faith in God was a light in my life, and now, after only forty-seven years, death had snuffed out this beautiful candle.

Now watching the funeral procession, I saw the young widow as she clutched her children's hands. The historic walk silenced a nation. My walk through God's Acre in Winston-Salem, North Carolina, was no less somber.

Our nation pivoted in a different direction. However, I was unaware of the national shift, only aware of my personal one. Lost in the fog of new grief, my Dad and I clung to each other. The rudder of our family ship was gone, and we drifted. Simple tasks became huge burdens. My grades plummeted, and Daddy barely shuffled through his job.

Each day I drifted downward into the pit of depression, poor test scores, and college-application rejection. I was on an island watching others live. Our grieving nation slowly recovered, but depression overwhelmed me. I needed care. An angelic, gray-haired doctor and his nurses supported me. A Virginia hospital was my private battlefield. Many prayer soldiers interceded for my health. Those prayers and the excellent care I received gave me a new life.

I would like to say I lived happily ever after, but life's trails are often rocky. I married a man with complexities like my own. Two children were born of our unsettled union. I continued to search for hope.

Depression again smothered me. Then, through a wonderful Bible study group, I found a Christian psychiatrist. Dr. Don treated me spiritually, emotionally, and physically. He gave me prescriptions for Scripture, journal writing, and medications.

"Where do you see yourself in your faith walk ten years from now? Where do you find your solace?" Dr. Don asked. He gave me Scriptures to memorize, including, "For God hath not given us the spirit of fear; but of power, and of love, and of a sound mind" (2 Timothy 1:7 KJV) and "Casting all your care upon him; for he careth for you" (1 Peter 5:7 KJV).

While that November morning of 1963 brought the death of my innocence, it also sparked the birth of my growing faith. It was an American Moment that would lead me on a U-Turn journey toward healing. I left Dr. Don's care with renewed purpose. My mother's faith was mine for the asking. My walk with God would give me the courage I'd seen in Jackie Kennedy. May 10, 1987, I received my long-awaited college degree. God filled my heart with, "I press toward the mark for the prize of the high calling of God in Christ Jesus" (Philippians 3:14 KJV).

WHEN NO JOBS EXISTED

by Jennifer Smith-Morris,
Valdosta, Georgia

In the heart of the Depression, lanky Howard, with his twinkling blue eyes and wavy brown hair, had already learned to live by his wits. His mother had left the family of ten when Howard was eight. His father couldn't care for all ten children, so at nine, Howard left home and lived with relatives, getting work wherever he could. By the time he was eighteenth, he knew how to work hard, stretch a dollar, and find hope in a bleak situation.

Howard was my granddad. I knew him as a man with sparse gray hair, but with the same lanky frame and twinkling blue eyes. He told me he'd always believed that God would provide. That was his faith: Granddad always asked for just enough—not too much and not too little, and his faith carried him time and again.

In 1934 Granddad was living in Wisconsin, where, like the rest of the country, there were no jobs. "Everywhere you looked, men were hungry and outta work," he'd say. Then the corners of his eyes would crease with a smile. "But I always managed to get some dinner."

Sometimes he would go to the diner that offered a Dime Plate dinner. He recalled, "I didn't even have the dime for the Dime Plate." He asked if he could wash dishes or scrub the grill for a plate of food.

He roamed the countryside. Sometimes he split wood at a farm, then knocked on the door and asked if he could do anything else to earn a meal. Sometimes he'd ask permission to sleep in the barn. "A little straw under my head, and I was pretty cozy for the night."

Men all over the country stood in lines, pleaded with factory owners, and struggled to avoid starvation and homelessness. Granddad heard a rumor that the local tannery needed workers. He started going each day to see if they had any jobs. Dozens had the same idea. "The room was packed. Just packed full of men."

Every day the foreman would squeeze out of the office door and announce that they had no jobs. He would return to the office and slam the door as the men filed out, heads low. Day after day Granddad left without work. This frustration must have deflated many. But it strengthened Granddad's resolve.

One day, weeks later, Granddad again heard the foreman make his announcement and again watched the room clear. Then he walked up to the office door.

"I figured the way to get some notice was to go on in there." So he stepped inside the dimly lit office and asked the foreman, "Did you really mean there aren't any jobs?"

With colorful language, the foreman assured Granddad that indeed no jobs existed. Granddad left smiling, returning the next morning to see if work was available. He never felt defeated. The obstacles he'd faced in his young life strengthened his survivor's spirit.

Many years later, he imparted this trait to his family: God will provide. He's faithful through all generations, just as the Psalm says. It was a matter of figuring out how the Lord would provide, and Granddad took it as a challenge to find out.

After several more daily visits, Granddad set off for the tannery as usual, ready to work, ready to go hungry, ready to see God work. But that morning, the tannery had an opening. Desperate men packed the room more tightly than ever. The office door swung open, and the foreman stood on a bucket and held up one finger. Shouts and arms raised as he peered at the crowd.

Granddad went into action, twisting through the crowd, aiming for the office door. He kept his head high, watching the foreman. The foreman surveyed the sea of faces then pointed his finger to my Granddad, yelling, "I want you."

And because of his tenacity, perseverance, and faith that indeed God would turn things around, my Granddad got that job even though no jobs existed.

A LEGACY

by Diane H. Pitts,
Wilmer, Alabama

Willard Huff, a U.S. Navy veteran of World War II, solves the world's problems every day during morning coffee breaks with old friends. His clear blue eyes twinkle as he finishes an escapade about a grandchild. Someone laughs and a hundred-watt grin splits his wizened face. And then something triggers a memory, and the years roll back just like the waves splashing the shores of the South Pacific islands. Suddenly he is telling a story about long ago.

"Before the war broke out, I volunteered. Even when they turned me down because of a burned hand, I went back two more times," Huff remembers. "I wrestled with God every time, knowing I was supposed to go. Finally the doctor waved me through, telling me that after a trip to the West Coast, I'd be sent back to the farm. But no one ever stopped me."

Huff remembers the U.S.S. *McCawley* leaving San Diego in 1943 for a thirty-day trip to the Solomon Islands, almost halfway around the world. While in the Pacific theater, he was helmsman of the flagship before the Solomon Islands' invasion. It was pitch black in those early hours before the battle. They were in uncharted waters—waters only God could navigate.

Right before daylight, as the bridge swarmed with officers and before general quarters was sounded, the admiral turned to Huff.

"Son, are you sure you can do this? You've got thirteen ships following you."

"I wish he hadn't told me that," Huff says in retrospect. "But I continued at the helm until the quartermaster took over for landing."

After depositing the marine and army forces, Huff's ship headed out. Just when Huff assumed his battle station on a twenty-millimeter anti-aircraft gun, enemy planes appeared, unloading torpedoes. Explosions from the boiler room rocked their gun, covering them with blinding steam. Somehow Huff survived that day, but the U.S.S. *McCawley* and sixteen of the five hundred crewmembers did not.

God had more work for Willard Huff. His next duty was aboard the *President Hayes*. Because of her record for landing troops, they received a navy commendation. Huff almost wasn't around to get it.

At Bogunsville, he was running one of the landing crafts. On one occasion they unloaded troops for hours under heavy enemy fire. On their final return they were getting underway when a rainsquall swept in. As sheets of rain engulfed them, Huff pointed the landing craft toward the ship. They came through the squall, appearing alongside the *Hayes*. Ready to hook on, Huff couldn't believe the captain motioned them away. Intent on getting the *Hayes* in formation with the other ships and not being left behind in the middle of the South Pacific, he forged ahead at ten to twelve knots.

Huff kept pace, repeatedly attempting to come alongside. Finally they hooked on. Although he feared disciplinary action, it never came. Once again, he survived. Once more God intervened.

In another incident he was awakened at midnight with orders to secure a cargo boom. Huff didn't want to send his men up in rough seas, so he went, taking along only one other sailor. The boat rolled as they cautiously crawled thirty feet up the swaying mast. The blackness covered their eyes like a mask so everything had to be done by instinct. Huff's heart pounded as the wind whipped their bodies around like rag dolls, even though they were tied on. He whispered prayers for safety.

Finally they secured the cargo boom. Huff's buddy crawled down first. As Huff stepped down, his foot slipped, leaving him suspended in mid-air.

"Time stood still as I swung above the waters, hoping the next pitch would bring back my foothold," Huff recalls. "It seemed like an eternity passed before my foot could anchor on. But it did. When my foot hit the deck, I promised myself I wouldn't go up high again, and I never did. Once again the prayers of this country boy were answered."

Slowly, the scene returned to the table, to the here and now of the coffee break. But every hand had gripped the helm. Everyone had been under gunfire. And everyone had felt the fear of the midnight on the mast.

My dad, Willard Huff, represents a generation of a different caliber. Lives will always be different because of the legacy this man and others leave: a simple faith in God translated into a lifetime of perseverance, honesty, and self-sacrifice. These traits are carved into the hearts and minds of their children and grandchildren.

A slightly different version of this story appeared in the February 24, 2002, edition of *The Selma Times Journal.*

A CHILD'S EXPLANATION

by Michelle Guthrie Pearson,
Leaf River, Illinois

I woke up at 6:45 A.M. when my son jumped into bed with me and said, "Turn on Buzz Lightyear, please!" We lounged for a few hours enjoying the morning cartoons before getting up.

Around 8:30 A.M., horrifying scenes took over the TV screen. News anchors looked for elusive words to describe the gruesome images. As I watched from the safety of my midwestern farmhouse, the World Trade Center towers collapsed. My four-year-old son asked, "Why are you crying, Mommy?"

"Because sometimes bad people do bad things, Sean. And this was a bad thing." I hugged him. "Sean, I love you so much, and I'm so glad you're here with me."

I made the beds, cleaned the kitchen, and hung laundry to dry. The television played during my household tasks, bringing developments of the tragedy. My son played in his bedroom, uninterested in the drama.

That evening, we heard the President speak about the need to have faith and trust in God and the need for our nation to unite. I saw touching scenes such as London's Buckingham Palace Guard playing "The Star Spangled Banner," and members of Congress singing "God Bless America" on the steps of the nation's Capitol.

More hard news about the tragedy continued. Feeling the need to get away from the television, I loaded my son into the car. Already, things were changing. A car drove by with an American flag draped over the back windshield and over the trunk. The flags at the fire station flew at half-mast. A sign outside a doctor's office asked people to pray for peace.

"Mommy, if everything happens for a reason, why did God let planes crash into those buildings?"

"I'm not sure, Sean," I answered. I knew his question had no simple answer.

We took lunch to the park. My senses were heightened as I noticed everything around me. The light scent of the prairie flowers, a butterfly landing on a cone flower, a brilliant blue dragonfly dancing with the summer breeze, the edges of autumn on the trees. These creations had always been there, but today I noticed them more than ever.

My son, whom I thought hadn't paid attention to the news, ran to me from the playground.

"Mommy, do you think God always wins?" he said, his big blue eyes focused on mine.

"What?" I replied.

"Do you think God always wins? Maybe the devil won this time. Maybe that's why something very bad happened."

"I don't know, Sean. The Bible says there is a purpose for everything under heaven. I'm just not sure we can understand what that purpose is right now," I told him. He wanted answers, but I didn't have any.

"Well," my son said thoughtfully, "maybe the devil didn't win. Maybe the devil made this happen, and God knew about it. But maybe God knew it would make people love each other more. You know, be nicer to each other, like last night on TV. Maybe He knew it would make people sing."

Sean's explanation made me think of one of my favorite Bible verses: Ecclesiastes 4:12: "Though one may be overpowered, two can defend themselves. A cord of three strands is not quickly broken."

Sometimes it takes a child to remind us to make a U-Turn and look to God for answers. Our faith and trust in Him will create a bond not easily broken by the enemy—in triumph or in tragedy.

UNCLE AL'S FLAG

by Mary Emma Allen,
Plymouth, New Hampshire

D on't we have a flag, Mom?" my daughter asked as we saw
so many flags flying after the September 11 attacks.

"We have Uncle Al's," I answered. "Wouldn't he be
proud to have his flag flown at a time like this when our
nation is facing one of its greatest tests?"

This flag had draped my uncle's casket. As a World War
II veteran who saw action in the Pacific, he was proud he had
fought to keep America free.

Uncle Al never talked much about those years on Guam
and the Pacific Theater as an aircraft mechanic. But he saved
his military uniform and gave instructions that he be buried
in it, with his medals pinned to his chest. I also found his
Bible that had traveled with him during those war years.

Three veterans had attended Uncle Al's funeral service and
spread the American flag over his casket. At the cemetery, they
folded and handed the nation's emblem to my mother, his
closest surviving relative. Mother passed the flag to me.

"Take care of Al's flag," she said.

Now, we pulled the flag out. My granddaughter looked
at it in awe and slowly unfolded the red, white, and blue
symbol of our country. She and her brother marveled at its
size. Then we hung it from the deck in front of our home.

I watched Uncle Al's flag ripple in the breeze as our country began to recover from the tragedy, and I called upon God
to help us find faith again. I thought it fitting that the flag
honoring a World War II freedom fighter now flew to honor

heroes who lost their lives during an act of war in 2001.

It seemed as if God was making us come full circle as we reexamined our faith. . .the faith that carried soldiers like Uncle Al through the days of World War II and strengthened our country after September 11.

HEROES

You need to persevere so that when you have done the will of God,
you will receive what he has promised.
HEBREWS 10:36

THE ULTIMATE CHALLENGE

by Marcia Knoblock,
Lawrenceville, Georgia

T -minus one minute and counting. . ."

I smiled as I heard the familiar announcement over the car radio. Local personalities chatted as Mission Control counted down the minutes and seconds until launch. Growing up in Central Florida gave me lots of advantages, including standing in my back yard to watch rockets launch from Cape Kennedy. Never mind that we were an hour away—we could see the plumes of smoke, and our excitement was as potent as if we were on the launching pad.

"Coming up on the thirty-second point in our countdown. T-minus thirty seconds. . ."

Now, years later, I was driving down the road as the shuttle *Challenger* was about to go up. I'd been away to college in Georgia, worked in Puerto Rico, and had ended up back home. This was my first opportunity in a long time to see a launch live instead of on television.

"T-minus 10. . .9. . .8. . .7. . .6. . .We have main engine start. . .4. . .3. . .2. . .1. . .and liftoff! Liftoff of the twenty-fifth space shuttle mission, and it has cleared the tower. . . ."

I turned into the parking lot just as the spacecraft pushed away from Earth. The normal sounds of the launch were comforting. We'd been to space fifty-five times in twenty-five years, and twenty-four space shuttle missions were in the history books. Number 25 was off to a good start.

"*Challenger,* go at throttle up. . ."

"Roger, go at throttle up," replied Dick Scobee, the

Challenger commander.

I was just pulling into a parking space when I heard the local announcer exclaim, "Something's wrong! The *Challenger* has exploded!" I sat, stunned. Then I heard it.

BOOM!

The sound of the explosion reached Central Florida just moments after it happened. I searched the sky for the familiar trail of smoke heading into the heavens, and found instead *Challenger's* trail ending in an ominous fork.

Hopes and dreams headed into the sky that day, only to return to earth as shattered as the space shuttle. A nation, lulled into complacency by success, was jolted awake by dismal failure. The adventure of space exploration had become commonplace, almost normal. No more.

That evening, President Reagan was scheduled to give his State of the Union speech. Instead, he addressed a nation in shock. He spoke of the first space tragedy nineteen years and one day earlier—the Apollo 1 launch pad fire that took the lives of Gus Grissom, Ed White, and Roger Chaffee. He reminded us gently, "It's all a part of the process of exploration and discovery. It's all a part of taking a chance. . . . The future doesn't belong to the fainthearted; it belongs to the brave."

At a memorial service for the *Challenger* crew, President Reagan added, "We learned again that this America. . .was built by men and women like our seven star voyagers, who answered a call beyond duty, who gave more than was expected or required, and who gave it with little thought to worldly reward."

"A call beyond duty. . ."

That's the kind of call that causes people to chase their passion. People as different as test pilots, career military men, scientists, and teachers. People as different as fishermen, tax collectors, doctors, and secretaries.

People as different as you and me.

A call is a call of destiny. We all have one, but will we listen? If we hear it, will we follow? And if we follow, will we be faithful "even unto death"?

The *Challenger* Seven heard the call to the stars. They listened and answered, knowing they were risking their lives, their futures, their families. They chose anyway, and became not a picture of defeat, but victory—the victory of embracing a call. . .and sometimes being required to pay its costs.

The call of Jesus still echoes: "Come follow Me."

Some hear it and ignore it. Some start but decide it's too hard or costs too much. Some even end up paying with their lives, as many of the original disciples and others can attest.

As I think back to the day the *Challenger* crew faced its greatest challenge, I hear Jesus' invitation in my ears. I can only say I will answer His call.

COURAGE THAT CHANGED THE WORLD

by Sandy Austin,
Lakewood, Colorado

The word "Columbine" represents tragedy, despair, and fear in our country. However, my strongest memory of Columbine is of courage. I was a counselor on the scene during the shootings and worked with students and parents for six months afterwards. My strongest impression of that whole time is of the courage of the young people.

Cassie Bernall and Valeen Schnurr boldly proclaimed their faith in God while looking down the barrel of a gun. Students stayed in the science room with their teacher, Dave Sanders, trying to save his life. More than seventy students sat crammed in the choir room office for several hours, while others huddled in the science lab, hearing the killers bragging three feet away on the other side of the door, not knowing if they would be the next victims.

Students risked their lives to pull their friends to safety. For three hours, wounded students in the library hung on for life, enduring the shrill fire alarm and water pouring from the sprinkler system, set off by the bombs. With their friends' bodies lying next to them, they wondered if help would come.

The day after the shootings, courage spread. At the crisis drop-in center, several students from a church youth group waited to get final word about their friend Cassie Bernall. Kara, one of the girls waiting, told me how Cassie had impacted her life and was her role model. Kara was devastated to learn Cassie was a victim. She clung to her friends while we shared Scripture and prayed. Kara said she was dedicating her life to keeping her faith in God strong, which is what Cassie lived and died for.

Two weeks later young people from a group, the Revival Generation, held a five-hour outreach for the teenagers in the local church. At the end of the evening a student using a cane exited the auditorium with three buddies. He had been an athlete, but now had an injured leg. The shooters' bullets changed his life. He was gasping as he approached the door. One of his friends took his cane, and another crouched in front of him. Swinging his arms to help, it took about a minute for him to climb on his friend's back. The simple move to get a piggyback ride took all of his strength. The other friend opened the door. The sports he had enjoyed and taken for granted will be only a memory now. His courage will have to last a lifetime.

Revival swept through Colorado's youth, and many took a bolder stand for their faith. That was clearly the case in other schools too. I saw it a few weeks later in my school, a few miles from Columbine, during a meeting for students trying to cope with a classmate's suicide. As they shared, one student, Angie, announced, "We need to pray. We need to pray right now!" We prayed, and she said, "This is serious stuff, and some of you guys might get mad at me, but I'm going to say it anyway. We all need to think about where we're going to go when we die—to heaven or hell. None of us knows when our last day will be, and we need to be prepared."

Angie had never been that bold before. I was cheering on the inside, silently saying, "You go, girl." No one mocked Angie.

The students of Columbine High School will be forever changed. Their faith impacted the world. We can learn from the courage of our youth.

Don't let anyone look down on you because you are young,
but set an example for the believers
in speech, in life, in love, in faith, and in purity.
1 TIMOTHY 4:12

Previously printed in *Stories for the Extreme Teen's Heart.*

FAITH AT IWO JIMA

by Nancy Cripe,
Minneapolis, Minnesota

Sergeant Jack Starr went ashore with his Fifth Marine Division on the black-ash beaches of Iwo Jima on February 19, 1945. The twenty-one thousand Japanese defenders holding the eighteen-square-mile sulfur island had gone into a labyrinth of caves. They waited until American troops had landed and piled their equipment on the beaches before pounding the Americans with artillery, rocket, and mortar fire.

Sergeant Starr and his comrades struggled over shifting and heavily mined sands toward garrisons in the rocky cliffs. The marines then began digging out the Japanese from sixteen miles of tunnels and fifteen hundred caves in hand-to-hand combat.

Five days into the battle, six marines raised the American flag atop Mount Suribachi. The now-famous photograph of the event won the Pulitzer Prize and was fashioned into a Marine Corp monument. Three of the six flag-raisers died on Iwo Jima.

Acre for acre, this island was World War II's bloodiest battle. One in three of the seventy-five thousand marines who went ashore was killed or wounded. Only one thousand of the Japanese survived.

"I have thanked God daily for His watch care and guidance over me, and it's a miracle that I'm still alive," Starr wrote his family on March 12, three weeks into the campaign that was supposed to have lasted three days. "We have just come off the lines after eight days. This is the second time we have come back, and we're just hoping we don't have to go back up." But twenty-one-year-old Sergeant Starr went back up.

The Allies needed Iwo Jima's three airfields to have a strategic airbase halfway between U.S.-held Mariana Islands and the Japanese mainland, 650 miles away. Short-range fighter escorts protected the long-range bombers during air strikes on the Japanese home islands. But these fighters didn't have the range of the big bombers and needed a refueling station. Crippled B-29s hit by enemy fire also needed a base for emergency landings.

Starr was a Minnesotan, one of seven children. He attended high school at Minnehaha Academy, a Christian school in Minneapolis. There, his classmate John Pearson became his close friend. Starr, the class president, and Pearson, the salutatorian, graduated in 1941. Each joined the service soon afterward, Starr as a marine paratrooper and Pearson as a navigator with the Army Air Force.

"It isn't the easiest thing to leave home, family, church and friends, but we have a job to do, not only for our country but for our Lord as well," Jack Starr wrote to his church. While in the South Pacific, he organized prayer meetings that grew from a handful of marines to large gatherings. "There is no greater privilege than helping a soul find peace in the Almighty, and that has been my privilege," Jack wrote. "God's way is the best way. I made Him my Commanding Officer, and Jesus never fails."

Lieutenant John Pearson became navigator of the Tamerlane, a B-29 bomber. The crew nicknamed him "Deacon."

Being Christians in the military also brought Starr and Pearson challenges. On Christmas night 1944, a discouraged

Jack Starr was "just going to give up; it seemed useless to try to tell the fellows about Christ because they just laughed at me." But then he prayed.

"About two minutes later, one of the boys called me outside. He said he could tell I had something he didn't have. He told me he wanted Jesus to come back into his life, so we prayed. I can't tell you how grand I felt inside. Helping that fellow turn back toward God was amazing. I could burst for joy to think that Jesus could work through me. Thank God, He can work through anyone who will let Him."

Sergeant Jack Starr went back up on the lines for a third time as the marines attacked Japanese defenses. Three days after writing his last letter home, Jack was killed in action on March 15, 1945. The news of his death reached home on Easter eve. "No matter what comes, my faith and trust are as solid as rock, and He will keep that which is committed unto Him," he had written his parents. "Remember, not 'good-bye,' just 'so long,' and God continue to bless our family as long as we stay true to Him."

The day after Starr's death, a B-29 returning from a bombing mission to Japan ran short of fuel. The plane was forced to land on Iwo Jima's Airfield No. 2, which was still under attack. The navigator who crawled out onto the runway was Lieutenant John Pearson.

John "Deacon" Pearson flew twenty-three B-29 missions, including a quartet that required emergency landings. After World War II he married, raised five sons, and served for thirty years as a Lutheran pastor.

Sergeant Jack Starr was buried with thirteen thousand World War II comrades in the Punchbowl, the National Memorial Cemetery of the Pacific in Hawaii. Admiral Chester Nimitz, commander of the Pacific Fleet, said of the marines' thirty-six-day assault, "Among the Americans who served on Iwo Island, uncommon valor was a common virtue."

Jack Starr believed in valor and sacrifice. But more than that, he believed, "Greater love has no one than this, that he lay down his life for his friends" (John 15:13).

THE FLAG RAISERS OF IWO JIMA

by Michael T. Powers,
Janesville, Wisconsin

Harlon Block died at the age of twenty-one with his intestines in his hands. That's what James Bradley told us at the Iwo Jima memorial. Each year my video production company goes to Washington, D.C., with eighth-graders from Clinton, Wisconsin. I always enjoy visiting our nation's capital, a place filled with the history of countless American Moments in time. But this fall's trip was especially memorable.

On the last night of our trip, we stopped at the Iwo Jima memorial. It is the largest bronze statue in the world and depicts one of the most famous photographs in history—the WWII image of the six brave men raising the American flag at the top of Mount Surabachi on the island of Iwo Jima, Japan. More than one hundred students and chaperones piled off the buses and headed toward the memorial. I noticed a solitary figure at the base of the statue. As I got closer, he asked, "Where are you guys from?"

"Wisconsin," I replied.

"Hey, I'm a Cheesehead too! Come gather around, Cheeseheads, and I will tell you a story."

As the kids gathered, the man began talking.

"My name is James Bradley, and I'm from Antigo, Wisconsin," he said. "My dad is on that statue, and I just wrote a book called *Flags of Our Fathers*. It's the story of the six boys you see behind me. Six boys raised the flag."

That's when he pointed to the guy putting the pole in the ground and told us his name was Harlon Block. "Harlon was an all-state football player. He enlisted in the Marine Corps with all the senior members of his football team. They were off to play another type of game, a game called 'war.' But it didn't turn out to be a game. Harlon, at the age of twenty-one, died with his intestines in his hands."

Bradley shared that detail because he said generals stand in front of the statue and talk about the glory of war. "You guys need to know that most of the boys in Iwo Jima were seventeen, eighteen, and nineteen years old," he continued. "Boys, not men."

He pointed again to the statue. "You see this next guy? That's Rene Gagnon from New Hampshire. If you took Rene's helmet off at the moment this photo was taken, you would find a photograph in the webbing. A photograph of his girlfriend. Rene put it there for protection, because he was scared. He was eighteen years old."

The next image of the statue was that of Sergeant Mike Strank, we learned. "Mike is my hero," Bradley exclaimed. "He was the hero of all these guys. They called him the 'old man' because he was so old. He was twenty-four. To motivate his boys in training camp, Mike didn't say, 'Let's go kill the enemy' or 'Let's die for our country.' He knew he was talking to boys. Instead he would say, 'You do what I say, and I'll get you home to your mothers.' "

The next man in the statue was Ira Hayes, a Pima Indian from Arizona who lived through the terror of Iwo Jima. "He went into the White House with my dad," Bradley explained. "President Truman told him, 'You're a hero.' "

Bradley said Hayes told reporters, "How can I feel like a hero when 250 of my buddies hit the island with me and only twenty-seven of us walked off alive?"

We learned Ira Hayes died drunk, face down, at the age

of thirty-two, ten years after the famous photo was taken.

"The next guy, going around the statue, is Franklin Sousley from Hilltop, Kentucky, a fun-lovin' hillbilly boy," Bradley continued. "Franklin died on Iwo Jima at the age of nineteen. When the telegram came to tell his mother that he was dead, it went to the Hilltop General Store. A barefoot boy ran that telegram up to his mother's farm. The neighbors who lived a quarter of a mile away heard her scream all night and into the morning."

Finally, Bradley pointed to the statue's image of his father, John Bradley. His dad lived until 1994 and had declined all interviews.

"When Walter Kronkite or *The New York Times* would call, we were trained to say, 'No, I'm sorry, sir, my dad's not here. He is in Canada fishing. No, there is no phone there, sir. No, we don't know when he is coming back.' "

In truth, Bradley's dad never went to Canada. Usually, he was sitting at the kitchen table, eating Campbell's soup. He didn't want to talk to the press because he didn't consider himself a hero.

"Everyone thinks these guys are heroes because they are in a photo and on a monument. My dad knew better. He was a medic. In Iwo Jima he probably held more than two hundred boys as they died, and when boys died in Iwo Jima, they writhed and screamed in pain."

Bradley recalled his third-grade teacher calling the elder Bradley a hero. "When I went home and told my dad that, he looked at me and said, 'I want you always to remember that the heroes of Iwo Jima are the guys who did not come back. *Did not* come back.'

"So that's the story about six nice young boys," Bradley finished. "Three died on Iwo Jima, and three came back as national heroes. Overall, seven thousand boys died on Iwo Jima in the worst battle in the history of the Marine Corps."

The number boggled my mind as I tried to comprehend how many lives those deaths altered back on American soil so many years ago. How many hearts of loved ones left behind were seared? Loved ones like this proud son who had so graciously shared part of his history with us.

Suddenly the monument wasn't just a big piece of metal with a flag sticking out of the top. It came to life before our eyes through the words of a son whose father was a hero then. . .and now.

THE LESSON OF LIGHT

by Kristine Vick,
Columbia, South Carolina

A dventuresome, fun-loving, outgoing, the perfect kid."
This is how one Columbine father describes his daughter, Rachel Joy Scott. The fifteen-year-old Columbine junior was one of the teens who died the day of the shooting. Like her name suggests, she brought joy to everyone who knew her. In her death, she touched many more lives.

Rachel was a committed Christian who often spoke about the Lord. She usually carried her Bible to school and spent quiet time each morning reading Scripture. Friends say she was always eager to share her faith. In one Columbine classmate's yearbook she wrote, "It's hard to find God in these halls, but don't lose faith because there is God in these halls. You just have to find Him."

Rachel kept a lengthy journal that was a window to her intimate thoughts. She wrote a lot about her spiritual journey and often wrote letters to Jesus asking Him to use her life. Her parents, Beth and Darryl, always knew the Lord would use Rachel, but never thought it would be through her death.

The day after hearing of their daughter's death, Beth and Darryl were emotionally spent, but seemed to be at peace. They said knowing their daughter knew the Lord was the one thing that would let them continue without being overwhelmed with grief. "I know God will work everything for the good," said Beth.

Nonetheless, both parents still felt a lot of anger. "I feel like I got robbed," Beth described. "Rachel was taken before her time. . .The enemy crossed that line. He deceived those boys [the gunmen], and they bought into the lie." Through heart-wrenching tears, she added, "I just thank God for letting me have her and love her as long as I did."

Rachel's funeral was broadcast on CNN to millions around the world. She was the first victim laid to rest. Hundreds attended the service. One by one, people told how Rachel's life had inspired them to be their best. They talked about a light that burned brightly inside her—a light they knew stemmed from her love for Jesus Christ. Without a doubt, they all knew she was now with the Lord, and despite their despair, Rachel was happy. Later, the minister invited those who wanted to give their lives to Jesus, as Rachel had done, to stand. More than half did.

I was in the church that day. I watched as people filed past her casket—family, friends, neighbors, and strangers. Many of them wrote a short note with an indelible marker on her white casket. One woman's tears spilled from her eyes as she tried to write her final sentiments to a girl she never even knew.

Rachel made all of us there—and many more watching on television—evaluate our own lives. Where do I stand with Jesus? What will people say at my funeral? Will I have eternal life? Have I let God use me? Is it time to make a U-Turn?

God used Rachel's death to teach us a lesson that will remain indelibly etched on our hearts and minds forever—the lesson of turning in commitment to Him.

THE PROMISED REUNION

by Susan Farr Fahncke,
as told by Charles Farrell, Southold, New York

A retired New York City firefighter, I attended more wakes and funerals last fall than I ever had in my lifetime. We buried our brothers whose lives were lost on September 11.

The first service I attended was for Vinnie, a firefighter, husband, and father of five young children. Soon after the funeral, Vinnie's wife learned she was in her first month of pregnancy. His wife feels this was a blessing from God.

Vinnie had delivered my newspaper when he was a young boy. His sister and my daughter are close friends. Vinnie also played an important part in my daughter's future. She attended a party Vinnie hosted and met one of his friends. That man became my son-in-law. My daughter said, "Everyone who knew Vinnie loved him."

Close friends of ours lost their twenty-nine-year-old son. Brian was a firefighter in Rescue I. He was missing from September 11 to November 26. The family prayed for seventy-eight agonizing days. In the beginning they hoped he would miraculously be alive in the rubble. Then they prayed only for recovery of his body. After going to Ground Zero to dig for his son's body day after day, Brian's dad realized they would be lucky to find a small part of his body. Still his parents prayed every day.

Somehow his father managed to get a video clip from the news, showing Brian among firefighters entering Tower II. The video showed a close-up of Brian. When his father showed it to us he remarked, "Look at that chubby face; look how he shows no fear." My wife and I could not hold back our tears.

The video lasted only a few minutes, but it was all the family had and all they might ever have. On November 26, the day before a planned memorial service, their prayers were answered. Brian's body was recovered—intact.

Brian was brought to the wake location at 10 P.M. the night before the service. A father was able to see his son one last time. The next day at the wake, as people asked Brian's father how he and the family were holding up, he answered, "A lot better now that God has answered our prayers, and Brian is back with his family."

Fire department chaplain Mychal Judge was on the scene shortly after the planes sliced into the towers. He blessed the firefighters as they entered the area. A poor soul who either jumped or fell from a tower floor high above struck down the first firefighter to die. Father Judge was immediately at his side administering last rites. That's when the first tower came down and Father Judge died. Firefighters dug him out of the rubble and took his body to the church across from the towers. They placed it gently on the altar. Then they returned to the dangerous, gruesome work.

I believe Father Judge led the long line of deceased to meet their Savior and spend eternity with Him. His faith put him into our Father's arms.

The proximity of these services made me recognize the similarity of bereavement. They all talked about the initial shock and feelings of powerlessness. As I attended these wakes, funerals, and memorials, I was apprehensive about what to say to the bereaved. At each service I left feeling peaceful from what they said to me about their own unfaltering faith in God.

The faces changed at each service. Wives, mothers, fathers, children, but the words were the same. Their common strength was their faith in God. This was no coincidence. The Bible tells us:

We need not sorrow as others who have no hope
For the Christian is promised:
An immediate reception in glory;
And a resurrection of the body.

But the Christian who dies doesn't only have certainty of an immediate reception in heaven. The Bible also promises a reunion with Christ and loved ones.

God will bring us all back together in His time.

FROM GRIDIRON TO GROUND ZERO

by Mary J. Dixon Lebeau,
Woodbury, New Jersey

N ick Brandemarti was a hometown hero. He was a football hero in the days when we chose our heroes on the
gridiron, not at Ground Zero. And he became my hometown's link to tragedy—just because he was at the right place,
but at the wrong time.

I didn't know Nick Brandemarti. We had attended the
same high school, but he was younger than I, but older than
my children. Still, I—like the other nineteen thousand people in West Deptford—anxiously watched the papers, checked
news links, and prayed for his safe return.

Our town had been united too many times by tragedy
in that year. In October, we mourned a twenty-three-year
veteran of the police force who was killed in a gun accident.
In March, we said good-bye to a courageous volunteer firefighter who clung to life for two months with burns over more
than 75 percent of his body. And next came September 11.

"Tomorrow's the memorial for Nick," my brother Mark
told me. We were standing in the house that we grew up in.
My brother, a teacher, knows most of the kids who graduate
from West Deptford.

"Did you know him well?" I asked.

"I coached him in track and football," Mark told me.
"Nick was a great guy."

Mark seemed to want to talk as much as I wanted to listen. He told me about the small, determined freshman
who—at only 110 pounds—was almost laughed off the field

when he showed up for football practice.

"Nick didn't have the size, but he had the determination," my brother remembered. "He had the heart."

Over the years, that heart served him—and our team—well. Nick grew into the role of star fullback. He worked hard, bulked up, and shaved seconds off his running time. By autumn 1996, Nick, a senior, was a team leader. Varsity co-captain. Voted "Best All Around." A scholar. An athlete. A good kid poised on the brink of growing up.

Those who love football in my hometown still talk about the Friday night that Nick—wearing number 44—scored four touchdowns, gaining 340 yards on twenty-five carries. Nick ran across the field and into the school's record books. Only two players in South Jersey history had carried for more yards.

The story is the stuff of high school legend, the kind of legend that has its roots on football fields throughout the country on chilly autumn Friday nights. The kind we whisper about over hot chocolate while watching this year's teams take to the field. The kind we tell our children about—just like my brother was telling me.

Nick Brandemarti's story is one of several thousand that ended in a New York minute. Surely each story is being etched into millions of memories surrounding this American Moment.

The Sunday of the memorial the church pews were jammed with those of us who knew where to turn when hope seemed lost. "For we know that when this tent we live in—our bodies here on earth—is torn down, God will have a house in heaven for us to live in, a home which He Himself has made, which will last forever," the priest said. We held onto each other and wept.

"We're retiring number 44 after this season," Mark later

said. "Even before he was lost in the tower, Nick was a hero here. He was a football hero, a leader on the field, a great guy."

And that is something to celebrate. Small reminders of life when we didn't worry about anthrax or enemy attacks. Back when our battles were on gridirons. Back in the day when stars on the football field glistened just as brightly as stars in the midnight sky.

THANKFULNESS

Give thanks to the Lord,
for he is good.
PSALM 136:1

THE BOMB THAT LAUNCHED OUR HEARTS

by Gayle Smith,
Oklahoma City, Oklahoma

How long does it take to change a life, a family, a school, a city. . .forever? On April 19, 1995, it only took one minute—from 9:01 to 9:02. A beautiful spring morning suddenly turned into the darkest day our city, Oklahoma City, has ever faced.

At 9 that morning, my husband, Myles, was at work. Our children, Tifani and Adam, were in school, and I was running errands. I was almost home when I saw billowy smoke in the distance, toward downtown. I called my husband, to see if he was downtown on business.

"All circuits are busy," the recording blasted through my ears with each call.

I hurried home to my TV and saw devastating pictures of our Federal building. It had exploded. Reporters were talking about a bomb. Our quiet state quickly became the focus of the world's attention. By noon almost everyone had heard about the Oklahoma City bombing.

Are they kidding? This is Oklahoma, I thought. *We're in the middle of the Bible belt. No one would want to bomb us.*

I finally reached Myles by phone. When I heard his voice, mine began to quiver. We decided Myles would check on friends and family, while I would call the school. The kids were taking achievement tests—all was calm there. But I was thankful when the children got home.

"Mom, what can we do?" they pleaded. "We have to help somehow." We began to think about how we could reach out to the city we call home.

That evening's dinner conversation focused on where we were and what we heard. My kids thought a school air-conditioner had blown. My husband thought it was a sonic boom, and I, a tire blowing. But somewhere in the discussion, the horrible event became too real when the phone rang and we learned a friend's husband was missing and a family from church was searching for their mother.

Myles's business companions at the social security office were missing, and within days, we learned the missing were dead. We grieved along with our friends, neighbors, city, state, and country. That day, 186 people died, including nineteen children.

My children organized a relief drive that stirred my heart. They put out fliers and called people, asking for anything from flashlights to food. Within days my garage overflowed with seventy-five hundred dollars in donated goods. We took carloads of items that could help people to distribution centers.

We said good-bye to many loved ones, friends, and coworkers as we laid them to rest one by one. But we focused on the Lord, seeking His peace, wisdom, and understanding. I'm thankful that God comforted those who lost so much. Thankful that when times are hard, Americans support each other. And I am thankful for yet another day to serve our Lord.

SAVED FOR SERVICE

by Lanita Bradley Boyd,
Fort Thomas, Kentucky

Jack Babel was sure breakfast was the best meal of the day aboard the U.S.S. *Detroit,* a light cruiser anchored in Pearl Harbor, Hawaii. After breakfast, he picked up his tray to return it to the cart of dirty dishes. Then his ears perked up as he heard the roar of a plane much too close for comfort.

Running up the stairs and onto the deck, he saw the sky filled with torpedoes and bombs and bright streaks of fire as the ground was strafed from above.

"Those are Japanese planes!" someone shouted.

"Man your battle stations!" the captain shouted. Jack scrambled into the crow's nest to report any other sightings. As he got into position, he looked across to the other side of Ford Island and saw the U.S.S. *Arizona* explode in a spray of fire, water, and debris. He grabbed the microphone and reported what he could see to his superiors. Japanese planes were still coming, and Jack hung on in the crow's nest with his binoculars trained on the horizon.

After awhile there wasn't much to report. A few American planes had taken off in pursuit, but the Japanese seemed to have temporarily pulled back. Finally, Jack took a deep breath. He'd responded to the emergency as he'd been trained to do. Now what had happened really hit him, and he realized how close he'd come to dying.

Looking back on that time, Jack now wonders why he didn't drop to his knees and thank God for saving him when so many died. Even though he certainly believed in God, faith just wasn't there. He shook in fear but did not even think of turning to God.

Throughout the next few days, word came of the deaths of those who were on the U.S.S. *Arizona,* the U.S.S. *Oklahoma,* and the three other ships that were sunk. Jack didn't know anyone who died, but hearing about the deaths of more than 2300 fellow Americans sickened him and made this eighteen year old more determined than ever to fight for his country

Soon he was transferred to the U.S.S. *Bowditch,* on which he went to the Bikini Atoll to set up a practice run for the A-bomb. During the next six years, Jack and his fellow soldiers patrolled many parts of the Pacific Ocean. Jack stayed in the navy until 1947, when he was honorably discharged. In 1949 he met a woman named Dorothy, now his wife of more than fifty years. Dot and others helped Jack meet Christ in a way that he'd never known. He now feels that God spared his life through all those years of conflict so he could know the saving grace of Jesus and make it the guide for his life.

Years of Bible study, church leadership, and evangelism have given him invaluable experiences and drawn him closer to his God. Now at age seventy-eight, Jack still serves in many ministries of his church—from Bible correspondence courses to children's outreach to recycling to finances. He is thankful that God spared his life at Pearl Harbor and made his service fruitful.

THE PREGNANT PAUSE

by Cay A. Gibson,
Sulpher, Louisiana

When I entered the living room, I casually looked at the TV set my husband had left on when he went to work that morning. The second airplane crashed into the second WTC tower. I was still trying to figure out what was going on and where these buildings were when my husband called. The employees in his company had heard rumors that America was under attack. I spent that morning going back and forth between the kitchen to answer phone calls and the living room to watch events unfold.

Still, I was blissfully ignorant of the magnitude of the events of September 11. I fed the children their breakfast, began homeschooling our third-grader, and started the laundry. When my husband came home early, I was relieved but continued my routine. We heard that President Bush had been flown to Louisiana. I panicked a bit about our safety. I didn't want the terrorists to come to our state to chase down the President.

That afternoon as I ran errands, I overheard a woman saying she was home with her two children, pregnant, and desperate for news about her husband. He worked at the top of one of the Twin Towers. I unexpectedly was drawn into this woman's agony because I was also pregnant and had small children at home. Suddenly, I felt a renewed sense of value for human life.

That sense of value for life lasted even though I spent much of the month defending why I was bringing a child into a world that had gone crazy with terrorism and fear. I was defiant with hope, saying, "War and terror are nothing new. The world has never been a peaceful place. A new baby is at risk from the moment of conception. And September 11, 2001, proved that all of our lives are at risk at every stage of life."

During the rest of my pregnancy, I held the calming knowledge that the world did go on, and that honor and freedom would triumph despite this recent attack.

But twenty days after my baby was born, I heard about the arrival of the daughter of flight 93 hero Todd Beamer. That plunged me into mass confusion. I mourned for Lisa Beamer as I thought of her raising a four year old, a two year old, and a newborn without the support of her wonderful Christian husband.

I mourned belatedly for all the victims and their families. I cried for the widows left to raise children as single mothers. I grieved for my baby brought into this barbaric world, and for the future of all my children. I suffered for the new mothers delivering and bonding with their babies in the absence of fathers lost in the attacks. I felt guilty taking my children to eat, sitting with the baby, and enjoying my meal, because my precious ones still had a daddy. I was hopelessly encased in postpartum depression.

So many families were still grieving for their loved ones while the rest of the world was getting on. Getting ready for the Winter Olympics in Salt Lake City, Utah. Debating the Enron scandal. Arguing about who was suing whom. All that while these families who had lost loved ones in the attacks were grieving.

Someone suggested that I should offer my pain to God, to somehow help ease the grief of those who had suffered such an enormous loss. That's when I made a U-Turn toward God and put everything into perspective.

I clung tighter to my husband and children in gratitude. I cherished the day, knowing tomorrow did not promise me this bounty. I prayed in thanksgiving that my husband had been present for the births of all of his children. I determined that if my husband lost his job as so many others did as a result of September 11, I would handle it with faith. I realized the most important things were that we had each other and our health. Everything else would fall into place. God would see to it.

I now feel I was blessed to have a baby after September 11. After a pregnant pause, God used my postpartum depression to raise my awareness of others' sufferings, and to fill me with more compassion than I had ever felt for strangers. He used it to deepen my thanksgiving for the gifts He had given me. God is sovereign, and His ways are not ours. I realized babies are God's rays of light and hope, no matter when they enter the world. They ensure that God's kingdom will triumph amid tragedy.

PENTAGON PLANE CRASH

by Major Glen A. Grady,
Alexandria, Virginia

The day many of us in the intelligence business have dreaded for so long finally came. Terrorism reached American shores.

I arrived at work just before 7:30 A.M. and learned a plane had hit the WTC. As I watched the television in my boss's office, a jetliner struck the second tower. I called my wife so she could turn on the television and follow the story.

A couple of hours later, I felt the building sway and then a rolling thunder grew very loud. A fireball followed and flames lashed against the windows on both sides of our office, a large, open area with cubicles. The main lights went out, and emergency lights kicked on. Alarms rang, but the water sprinklers never activated.

We quickly realized this wasn't a bomb, but was probably a plane. Later I discovered that my office was directly over the fuselage and we were right above the impact point. No doubt the construction design by the engineers kept us alive.

Smoke filtered through the office and we started, calmly and orderly, to move into the center courtyard, which would be the safest place—any second aircraft would probably hit the outside again. In the courtyard we started to account for everyone in our office. Injured were brought out, people in bloody uniforms were wandering, and people were wrapped in sheets. The building authorities moved us into the south parking lot, where we again fanned out to find everyone in the office.

Eventually the police moved us farther away to establish a five-hundred-yard perimeter around the building. A small cheer went up as the first F-16 roared by at a low altitude over the Pentagon.

As I joined thousands of other evacuated people, my foremost thought was to contact my wife. I knew she would be terrified from watching the TV reports. She would realize the impact of the jet was near my office. Finally, after about three hours, I reached her from a pay phone.

Over time, the crowd dissipated as people began to try to make their way home. After rallying with our team in a nearby apartment and learning the official word that by the grace of God, we had positive accountability of everyone in our office, I called my wife to let her know I would start trying to make my way home. We piled into the crowded metro. By now the roads were jammed, and D.C. was a mess, as people headed home en masse.

When I reached the metro stop where I'd parked my car, I took two people in my office home because they had left their car keys in their desks. At about 3 P.M. I was finally home. I gave baby Noah a big hug when I got in the door. My wife had been on an emotional roller coaster. The phone had been ringing all day, and she had to deal with almost losing me. We were overjoyed to see each other.

This event is the closest I have ever come to facing my mortality, and I can say the sunset at twilight never looked more beautiful! My heartfelt thanks goes to those in the Pentagon working near me, who gave their lives to protect my freedom. A verse from the Bible rings so true: "The greatest love is shown when people lay down their lives for their friends" (John 15:13 NLT).

At a prayer vigil service at our church, I praised God:

In spite of this awful, mixed-up day, You are still on the throne, and I know that Jesus is coming again! I don't have all the answers regarding the attack, but I know that God loves us and that His hand was at work in my life on September 11. I learned God is in control and we can trust Him.

The Lord has made the heavens his throne;
from there he rules over everything.

PSALM 103:19 NLT

MOMENTS OF
FORGIVENESS

Forgive whatever grievances you may have against one another.
Forgive as the Lord forgave you.
COLOSSIANS 3:13

UNEXPECTED TRAGEDY, UNDESERVED GRACE

by Kathy Whaling,
Littleton, Colorado

April 20, 1999, was my wedding anniversary. I couldn't wait to spend the evening with my husband at a romantic dinner and movie. I started the day by heading to the health club with my friend Sharon, and then I went shopping at a local store.

I had picked out a few items to purchase when my name was paged. Sharon was calling. She'd just gotten home from the health club and sounded terrified, talking about a shooting at Columbine High School where my three daughters attended.

Sharon lived behind the school and heard gunshots and bombs. She had looked over her backyard fence and had seen screaming students running out of the school.

Everything will be okay, I thought. *Sharon was probably overreacting.*

I raced home and turned on the television. I saw my children's high school with terrified, crying students still running out. This couldn't be real! But the helicopters flying over my house, the neighbors coming over, and people calling reinforced the reality.

Two of my three daughters, Stephanie and Chanelle, called, crying frantically, to let me know they were all right. When my husband, Bob, pulled into the driveway with Heather in the passenger seat, I breathed a sigh of relief. All three girls were safe.

Later that evening, the girls screamed with gut-wrenching

cries when they learned some of their close friends had been killed. Cassie Bernall had given Chanelle a ride home from youth group the Sunday night before. Rachel Scott, Stephanie's good friend, was dead. Heather had enjoyed sitting next to Isaiah Shoels on the bus every day because he was always happy and funny and brightened her day. My children attended four funerals in five days—the first funerals they had ever attended. I felt helpless. No kisses, candy-flavored pills, or cartoon Band-Aids could alleviate their pain.

As days passed, the shock wore off. But anger replaced it, and my hostility affected my behavior. My family felt as if they were walking on eggshells. To this point, I had lived with the illusion that I could handle any crisis. After all, I was "Super Mom"! Not anymore. I had lost control. I felt inadequate as the nurturer of my family. Frightened, I needed to be nurtured myself.

In this fragile state, I sought God. I had been a compromising Christian, but now I began to pray. I sensed that God wanted me to get the girls into Christian counseling and got a referral from my church. When I called Dee Dee to set up appointments, she suggested I make an appointment for myself as well.

"Not right now," I said. "Let's take care of the girls. Maybe we'll fix me later."

As weeks passed, God brought hope back into my girls' lives and drew them closer to Him. Their fears diminished while their faith in God increased. I was overwhelmed to see God work in their lives. I had thought it was my job to fix everyone, but now I saw I didn't have to do it all by myself. After a few weeks, God softly said, "Now it's your turn."

Well, all right, God, I'll go see Dee Dee, but nothing is really wrong with me now that my kids are doing better, I thought. At my appointment, we chatted about the girls. Then she asked, "How do you feel about the Columbine incident?"

I told her I was angry. . .not so much at Eric and Dylan, but with their parents. "How could they not know what their kids were doing? How could they not know their kids were troubled? How could they let their sons put my daughters through this horror.? How dare they!"

Dee Dee understood my anger but gave me a choice of two responses to move beyond that place. I could write a letter to the Harris and Klebold families, telling them how I felt. Or I could do what God wanted me to do—forgive them. She said it would be a gift I could give to God and in return, God would bless me.

You want me to forgive just like that? The letters seemed like an easier choice, but I knew God wanted me to work toward forgiveness. The next morning as I prayed, I asked, "Father, why should I forgive these parents whose sons have put my children through such trauma?"

The Lord answered, "My dear child, I have forgiven you of the same sins. Don't point at the speck in someone else's eye, when you have a log in your own."

God reminded me of sins of my past that I had tried to forget. I asked God to forgive me for harboring such anger and bitterness. I forgave these parents, and for the first time thought of what they must be facing. Something wonderful happened as I made a U-Turn from blame to forgiveness. God replaced my anger with wonderful peace. I had never felt anything like this.

During my next visit with Dee Dee, I told her what God had done. And knowing I could trust her, I told her about those hidden sins of my past—saying the words aloud for the first time. I told her I'd had an abortion twenty years ago. . .

and then another one ten years later.

Dee Dee listened to my terrible past compassionately. Then she told me about a God who never intended for me to live with this guilt I'd harbored for twenty years—a God who doesn't condemn those who are forgiven in Christ. Now I realized how desperately I wanted to have my broken life "fixed."

Dee Dee told me to write a letter to each baby. She said God would give me their names. I spent the next three days thinking about the babies' names. I wondered whether they were boys or girls. Then God spoke to my heart. "Jeremiah and Joshua."

The next day I wrote a letter to each baby. I poured out my grief and asked my babies to forgive me. I told them how I anticipated being reunited with them in heaven. Even though it was difficult to write the letters, I felt relieved afterwards and comforted by Jesus (Matthew 5:4).

The next day I told Dee Dee that after twenty years of guilt, I was ready to give the pain to God. We prayed. I told Jesus how sorry I was with tears streaming down my face. Then I could envision Jesus with my babies—Joshua in one arm and Jeremiah in the other. I knew Jesus had set me free.

Writing those letters was the hardest thing that I had ever done, but the blessing was worth it. I have learned the most important thing in living the Christian life is to fully depend on God. I now know that God is in control—not me. I've never felt so much peace, even through the storms. I'm thankful God used the heart-wrenching situation at Columbine to bring my daughters closer to Him and to set me free. My God is capable of turning tragedy into triumph. Thank You, Lord, for U-Turns!

THE SLAP

by SuzAnne Martin,
Naples, Florida

I n the fall of 1963, my world revolved around sororities, University of Texas football, an overprotective father, and Texas politics. I had worked in campaigns since 1958. My first job was licking stamps in the campaign office of a city council member. In the Texas campaign headquarters of John F. Kennedy in 1960, I answered phones and recruited voters. In 1962 I was a speechwriter for John Connally's gubernatorial campaign. My political career was well on its way. I was nineteen, and life was good.

Then my boyfriend Tom invited me to go skiing in California during the Thanksgiving break. I convinced Dad I would be home in time for Thanksgiving, study, be chaperoned by Tom's parents, go to church, and not compromise the family's virtue.

Keeping my word, I went to church with Tom and his parents. Monday afternoon I tried snow skiing for the first time. I was determined to conquer all obstacles, at least on the bunny slopes. After all, I'm a Texas girl bred and born, and unconquerable.

Tom's friends were delightful and gave me skiing hints. They teased me about being a Texan, but I took it in stride, because Texans are Texans first and then Americans.

On Friday morning, I had just come down to the kitchen when I heard the announcement on the radio: "The president has been shot while riding in an open motorcade. Also shot was John Connally, governor of Texas."

My perfect world was gone. Those lethal bullets in Dallas careened across the miles to explode my world. John F. Kennedy—my role model, my president—dead by an assassin's bullet. John Connally—my boss, my mentor, my governor—injured.

During the day, we talked little. In the evening we gathered. As we talked, moods changed. At one point, a young woman said, "Of course, this would only happen in Texas; they still live in the Wild West."

Tom's brother added, "Texans are a bunch of rednecks. We should just put a huge fence around the state and send all the criminals there to live."

"Wait a minute, I'm from Texas," I protested.

Without warning, the girl who'd spoken first slapped my face. Tom took me outside and tried to comfort me. But I could not be comfoted.

How can this be happening to me? Why did she hit me? I wondered. *Oh, God, why am I here in California with people I don't really know?* I couldn't hear God's answers—only more questions.

Over time, I began to absorb perspective on the events. Slowly, my routines continued. Sororities, football, Texas politics, and an overly protective father. The innocence never returned, but the replacement was acceptable. My world once again was full of good things. But the sting of the slap was there too.

Forgiveness was an alien concept to me. Every newsreel, every discussion on theories, and the countless reruns of that young lad saluting—each incident overwhelmed any glimmer of forgiveness.

One Sunday ten years later, in church with my husband and two young sons, I opened the bulletin. I saw forgiveness in a quote from John F. Kennedy: "And so, let us not be blind to our differences, but let us also direct attention to our common interests and to the means by which the differences can be resolved. And if we cannot now end our differences, at least we can help make the world safe for diversity. For in the final analysis, our most basic link is that we all inhabit this small planet. We all breathe the same air. We all cherish our children's future. And we are all mortal."

As I read that quote, the slap, the pain, and doubt disappeared—replaced through God's grace with forgiveness. He gave me the explanation that spurred my U-Turn of forgiving in the church's Sunday bulletin.

THE WALL

by Iris E. May,
Ulster, Pennsylvania

B ill kicked the pebble, sending it onto the next lawn. He glowered, murmured, and swore under his breath. "Why don't they have signs telling you how to get there? It's not supposed to be a secret."

We had walked for an hour up and down Pennsylvania Avenue in Washington, D.C.

I pointed. "Let's try over there."

Finally we found the line leading to "The Wall." It wound its way back at least a quarter-mile. The closer we came, the more agitated Bill became. A park volunteer handed him a directory. He skimmed through it.

"How am I supposed to find anyone with this stupid thing?"

"Let's ask someone to help us," I suggested.

He glared at me. Then he blurted, "How am I ever going to find my unit? Why couldn't they list them by units?" He ran his hand though his hair and kicked an imaginary stone.

"Honey, what's the matter?"

He almost roared. "I can't remember their names! How can I find them if I can't remember their names?"

I laid my hand on his arm. "I'm sorry."

"Why can't I remember? I ate with them, slept with them, and held some while they died." He drew a deep breath. "Now I can't remember their names." He hung his head.

My strong, sensitive husband was crying. I ached with pain for him. A gentleman, several people ahead of us, dropped back and stood beside Bill, though he never looked directly at him. "When were you there?"

Bill glanced up. "1969."

"I was '68–'69. You been here before?"

"No. You?" Bill quizzed.

"Yeah, many times."

His shoulders slumped forward, his hands slipped into his baggy coat. He shuffled his feet, staring at the ground. Then he looked over the park, his eyes blank.

Bill's face held the same look.

"I can see their faces. I can hear them screaming with fear and pain even in my sleep," the man said. He wiped his hand over his eyes. "Sometimes I come here and stay all day. They don't seem so loud from here. Like I'm closer and they don't have to yell so loud, you know?"

"Can you remember their names?" Bill questioned.

"Only a few. Their eyes, their broken bodies, but not their names."

"I thought it was only me. I feel terrible. I'd hope someone would remember my name, but I can't remember theirs."

"Yeah, me neither. While I was over there, I got so I would not learn names. It didn't hurt so much for some unknown to die, but a friend? I lost too many and became hard on purpose."

"Me too," Bill nodded. "I'd just learn a name, a little about his family, and he'd get shot."

Neither asked nor volunteered names here either.

When we stood beside the wall, Bill reached out and traced names with his finger. "I wonder if he was one?"

We worked our way around the corner. Suddenly Bill exclaimed, "Here they are! This was the squad that almost got wiped out. We came in from a two-day patrol and waved to them on their way back out." He choked. "I never saw most of them again."

"Gomez, Hector, Smith, Smith. . ." He read the names, touching each with his finger. He knelt by the spot and put his head against the wall. When he stood, he turned to me and started talking.

"We called this one Small Fox because he crawled in the tiniest holes."

He'd point to another name and tell me what he remembered. Mostly nicknames, or hair color, or a strong southern accent. One had dried squid sent from Hawaii. The buried memories now rolled from Bill's mind.

I stood silently. Listening. Praying God would turn Bill's mourning into gladness, sorrow into comfort and joy. He'd held twenty-six years of grief. Maybe now the hatred would be released. With God's help he would finally be at peace.

That visit to the wall did free him. I watched my dear husband make a U-Turn from hate to hope, from horror to healing. Today he freely talks about his experience in Vietnam. God gave him peace.

FORGIVENESS AT PEARL HARBOR

by Susan Farr Fahncke,
Kaysville, Utah

L ast March my husband and I spent our anniversary in
Hawaii. One of the sights I was most eager to see was the
Pearl Harbor memorial. As we waited for our group's turn
for the tour, Marty and I heard that a survivor of the bombing would speak in the courtyard. We hurried over to listen.

Dr. Joe Morgan, still handsome at seventy-nine, spoke
softly but intensely as he described the nightmare attack of the
Japanese on Pearl Harbor. Joe had been stationed on the southwestern shore of Ford Island, right in the center of Pearl
Harbor. That Sunday morning, he'd pulled duty in Aircraft
Utility Squadron Two. At 7:55 A.M., he heard the planes div-
ing. At first Joe assumed they were the usual planes that came
before the aircraft carriers.

Then the bombing began.

The nineteen-year-old Texan was confused by the .25-
caliber machine gun bullets that rained down around him.
He watched fellow sailors fall, hit and bleeding. His confusion turned to horror and fear. He heard an explosion on the
runway and looked up. He saw the symbol of the rising sun
on the plane and realized the Japanese Imperial Navy was
attacking them.

Joe's first instinct was to hide. But seeing other young
men scramble for weapons, he felt ashamed of himself.
Running outside to face his attackers, Joe saw an abandoned
machine gun and took up his post, shaking in his number
eight shoes.

Filled with a deep fury, Joe fired and shot down Japanese

planes. Although Joe was a Christian, he was unable to shake off the hatred he felt for the nation that was so shockingly killing many young American men. The battle finally ended, with 2,403 Americans killed. The men didn't know if the Japanese would return, so Joe and others stayed at their posts all night. During the night, Joe said a prayer that changed his life. He promised God that if he survived that war, he would become a preacher.

The attack on Pearl Harbor changed Joe's life. Although he kept his word to God, he never quite overcame his feelings for the Japanese nation. Joe eventually became pastor of the Wailuku Baptist Church in Maui. Two years later, Mitsuo Fuchida came to the island. He was commander of the naval air forces that led the attack on Pearl Harbor, beginning with Ford Island, on December 7, 1941. Fifteen years had passed since that attack, but Joe still had mixed feelings. After much turmoil, Joe decided to go and listen to Commander Fuchida. He heard Fuchida tell of becoming a Christian. After Fuchida's talk, Dr. Joe Morgan introduced himself.

Mitsuo Fuchida bowed and said one word, "Gomenasai." He said simply, "I am sorry."

What happened next was as important an American Moment as any other in history. Fuchida reached out to shake Joe's hand. As Joe clasped his former enemy's hand, he realized all the anger and animosity toward this man and his country were gone. God had replaced them with forgiveness. Joe Morgan and Mitsuo Fuchida shook hands as brothers in Christ.

Tears filled our eyes as Marty and I listened to this incredible U-Turn story of forgiveness. Once the two men were shooting at each other. Now, brothers in Christ, they would fight common foes: hatred and unforgiving hearts. A U-Turn that, God willing, will continue for generations to come.

NAZI POW #2458

by Kari West,
Pleasanton, California

> *The thrill of combat got into my blood; but the Army-Air*
> *Force didn't cover what the jerk of a parachute strap felt*
> *like, nor did they tell us what a German burp gun looked*
> *like. I never dreamed of how it would be to march six hun-*
> *dred miles like a foot soldier, with a bayonet at my back.*
> *The sudden jerk of my harness knocked all of the training*
> *out of me, and I didn't know if I could survive it.*
>
> DONNELL F. MILLER

It was the coldest winter on record. Snow covered the dirt and blanketed the roof tops at Kriegsgefangenenlager der Luftwaffe—a German prisoner of war camp near the Baltic Sea that housed ten thousand noncommissioned officers in four compounds of ten barracks each. Inside Room 5 of Barracks 10, Stalag IV, you could see your breath. Twenty-year-old staff sargeant Donnell Miller shivered in his bed. The coal-burning stove in the middle of the room labored to keep up with the chill—when there was fuel.

Dog tired from a fitful night of adjusting to his shifting bed—slats topped by a sagging gunnysack mattress of wood shavings—Don awaited lunch's lukewarm bowl of potato soup. Breakfast had been the usual cup of hot water, while supper was always a bowl of steamed potatoes. Occasionally, a mildewed loaf of whole grain bread and sawdust arrived. "When we looked outside and saw the sawdust blowing off the bread, we got out the cards and started shuffling," said Don, describing how the loaf was divided among the twenty-four men. "The high card meant you got first choice; the low card meant crumbs; but nobody squawked."

The men also lived on rumors. They gleaned information from new prisoners, from ministers and priests traveling from camp to camp, and from secret radio operators inside the camp, who bribed guards for parts to manufacture a radio to retrieve BBC broadcasts out of London. "Guys were sent from barrack to barrack with the news; but in the passing, it became distorted," said Don.

For eight months, Don was a POW. Hidden among his possessions was a rumpled Gideon New Testament, a gift from his best buddy, that he normally kept in his left-breast pocket. Bearing an inspection stamp on the first page, it was still intact despite the leather cover being ripped apart during a search. On his feet were rather worn shoes that he had tied to the harness of his parachute when they were shiny and new. At the time he never imagined the role these two possessions would play in the days ahead or how the values and faith that his family had passed down to him would help him survive this American Moment in history.

Donnell Miller came from tough pioneer stock. His great-great-grandfather died on the Oregon Trail, and his twelve-year-old great-grandfather drove the wagon the rest of the way. During the Depression, his schoolteacher father made a living the best he could and taught Don accountability for his actions. Only fifteen years old when his father died, Don worked evenings and Saturdays to help his mother. He lived in the garage so she could take in boarders.

In January 1943, he was drafted into the Air Force in Oakland, California. Trained as a radio operator, he joined the 493rd Bomb Group, 861st Squadron, in Debach, England, on May 15, 1944. His job aboard a B-24 was to call the Army

Airways Communication stations en route with a position report, direction, and estimated time of arrival. On D-Day, June 6, 1944, the squadron flew its first mission designed to hit strategic targets in France. They were to bomb bridges and routes the Germans counted on to defeat the Allied invasion and landings at Normandy and Omaha Beach. Above the clouds, flying in tight formation at twenty thousand feet with no visibility, Don tossed bails of tinfoil out the window to throw off German radar. Black puffs of smoke dotted the sky and hot fragments of steel rattled the aluminum skin of the plane.

Suddenly, the nose gunner screamed, "Aircraft falling at two o'clock!" Don watched a bomber from the left wing of the lead squadron collide with another aircraft. Sick to his stomach, he saw tail assemblies, wings, and engines spinning in all directions—but no parachutes. "All I could do was pray for the safety of the men, committing each man's life to the will of God," he said. "In a few seconds, twenty of our buddies were gone."

Don's personal Day of Infamy came a week later during his third mission. On June 14, after releasing bombs and being hit by 88 mm fire, the B-24 suddenly lost altitude. The right outside engine sputtered as gasoline poured over the wing. "I looked out the window and saw the White Cliffs of Dover," said Don. About fourteen thousand feet over the English Channel, the pilot ordered the crew to bail out.

"I had never parachuted, even in practice," Don said. "I just squatted and hopped off the catwalk, twisting myself towards the rear of the airplane. I waited until I dropped below the tail of the bomber, then pulled the rip cord."

The wind blew Don toward France. He landed in a two-foot-high barley field, avoiding a farm house roof and barbed wire fencing but striking his foot on a rock. Amazed that only his ankle was injured, he ripped off the sheepskin boots required in the plane, untied the shoes from his harness, and laced them tightly to his swollen feet. He was glad to be alive.

For three hours, Don hopped on one leg, avoiding capture, as German soldiers combed the barley fields. "Fear gripped my soul," Don said. "I asked the Lord to give me the strength to take whatever was coming. I knew things were going to get a lot tougher."

And things did. He was captured, and after weeks of solitary confinement and intense interrogation, he ended up in Stalag IV. Yet for Don, the low point of the war didn't come until the end of January 1945 after the Battle of the Bulge, as he watched thousands of prisoners—mostly Russian and French—stagger into camp. In freezing rain, they dug through trash piles for rags to clothe themselves or wrap around their bare feet before returning to the road. Rumor had it that the Red Army was advancing from the north, seizing everything in its path, and overrunning camps. Don wondered if the thunder in the distance was gunfire.

"As I watched these poor souls and their weary guards hobble out of camp, I was scared to death," he said. But despite his apprehensions, Don knew he was not alone; that the same God who had been with him in the past would be with him whatever happened. The dog-eared New Testament reminded him of that.

Late one night, a guard burst into the barracks and said, "Get ready. Tomorrow morning at 8 A.M. we're out of here. Take what you want. We aren't coming back." In less than twelve hours, 240 guys ripped up their long johns and created knapsacks for the journey. Escorted by armed guards and German shepherd dogs, the prisoners walked, carrying everything they owned on their backs and wearing every piece of clothing they had, including their heavy GI coats. For an hour they walked full speed over dirt roads pockmarked with ruts before weariness forced them to abandon nonessentials. Don realized his daily workouts and walking had paid off. Even though his feet were blistered, and his shoulders caved in, he kept his food and the meager possessions he had brought from camp.

"We walked for three months straight—six hundred miles —in twenty-degree-below-zero weather, staying in barns at night and living on whatever food we carried from camp and an occasional potato," said Don. "A lot of guys died. I don't know how I made it through, except the Lord had something for me to do."

Don Miller weighed 180 pounds when first captured but only 115 pounds when the British liberated him on May 2, 1945, in Kittletze, Germany. Don admits that for years he hated the Nazis and blamed the POW camp commandant for violating the Geneva Convention. "Now I realize we were destroying our own supply lines by our bombing," he said. "I'm not angry anymore. And I have no worry because I'm right with Jesus."

Today, seventy-nine-year-old Don Miller looks back and sees God's hand in every detail of his life—from his marriage to Julia, whom he met in 1945 and with whom he raised two children; to the construction business he owned and the Bible study he taught for twenty-five years. He speaks of the ground he covered in those worn-out shoes, that rumpled pocket New Testament that he still has, and the verse that sustained him through the horror of war—"For he shall give his angels charge over thee, to keep thee in all thy ways. They shall bear thee up in their hands, lest thou dash thy foot against a stone" (Psalm 91:11–12 KJV). Nazi POW #2458 credits his survival to God's grace.

ANGELS AMONG US

Clothe yourselves with compassion, kindness,
humility, gentleness and patience.
COLOSSIANS 3:12

GUARDIAN ANGEL ON DUTY

as told to Mary A. LaClair,
Vernon, New York

W hen I first saw the hole in the heart of our nation's
security, the Pentagon, my first thought was Faye!

My friend Faye had just moved to Maryland be-
cause the daughter she lived with had gotten a job at the
Pentagon. Faye and I had been friends since she'd attended a
Bible study I taught.

I immediately dialed Faye's number. "Where is your
daughter? Has Sheila started working yet?" I asked.

"Today was the second day at her new job in the Pentagon!" Faye told me, terror edging her voice. "We haven't
heard from her."

"Okay, I'll pray too," I promised. "Let me know."

The next day I heard the amazing story. Sheila was sitting at her desk, trying to sort out the confusion of her new
responsibilities, when a fireball exploded next to her desk.
Then the room went dark and filled with smoke, fumes,
noise, and confusion. She gasped for air and tried to run
away away from the desk.

At that point, Sheila realized her hands were on fire. She
tried to break a window, but it wouldn't budge. Fortunately
she remember the first rules she'd always been taught in fire
safety. Get down low and stay low. She fell to the floor. Her
throat burned, but the air was a little lighter.

Sheila knows God. She cried out, "God, help me find a
way out of here. I can't believe You brought me here to die
like this."

God calmed her spirit when she suddenly heard a man's voice. The smoke in her lungs blocked her from speaking, so she clapped her painful, burned hands, hoping he could follow the sound. He did. She heard the fire extinguisher. He put out the flames on her hands. Then he grabbed her arm and led her out of the E section of the Pentagon, close to the point of impact.

On the national TV news that night, I saw my friend Faye at her daughter's bedside in the hospital. "I pray for my daughter every day, as I do for my other children," Faye testified.

"My guardian angel saved me," Sheila explained. "I didn't get a good look at him, but I remember thanking him after we got outside. When I looked back at the building, I was amazed I got out of that inferno. Jesus clearly saved me."

When Sheila was released from the hospital, she still needed plastic surgery on her face, hands, back, and legs. Her husband, a volunteer firefighter, was joined by other firefighters and police officers to give Sheila a royal welcome home.

A white limousine awaited her. Fire trucks extended their ladders in an arch, decorated with flags, to line part of her route home. Red, white, and blue balloons adorned the journey. Local media cheered her on. But the best part was seeing her family.

"I was blessed to have another day to see my husband and children," Sheila says. "My heart aches for other victims whose families won't be able to hug them and say 'I love you.'"

AN ANGEL IN THE CLOSET?

by Renie Szilak Burghardt,
Doniphan, Missouri

n June 1944, my family and I were on the move, as were the troops of a distant land called America. Their move-ment on Normandy would result in victory and end the war the following year. I did not know I would owe much of my future happiness and safety to America.

I was born in the Bacska region of Hungary, on the Serbian border, which no longer exists. After Tito came into power in 1945, Bacska became part of Yugoslavia.

In 1944, as the war intensified and Tito's Communist Partisans (guerillas) closed in on the region, my grandpar-ents, who raised me, decided to move to a safer area. So, one early fall morning, we were in our horse-drawn wagon packed with some of our belongings. We had to leave behind many familiar and dear possessions.

My cat, Paprika, and I snuggled in the wagon bed. Hund-reds of other wagons were on the road, seeking safer places. But safe places were hard to find. Often, when we heard war planes, we would scramble out of the wagons and run for cover in the nearest ditch, hoping those silver cigars wouldn't drop bombs on us! At night we would set up camp on the roadside, build-ing fires and cooking meager suppers, before trying to sleep.

We finally settled in Zirc in upper Hungary. For awhile we felt safe. Christmas that year was meager, but we cele-brated. We had a small, candle-lit Christmas tree, and under it were mittens, a new red hat, and a scarf that Grandma had knitted for me by unraveling her old sweater. My most prized gift was a jumbo orange my grandfather somehow found.

The day after Christmas our safe world shattered. War-planes approached the city. Sirens went off. The air filled with the deafening roar of exploding bombs. Our house shook.

"Run into the closet!" an inner voice urged me. Terror-stricken, I ran while my grandparents followed. As I reached the closet, I sank into a corner, covering my ears. I closed my eyes so tightly I didn't think they would ever open again.

"Sweetheart, everything will be all right," my grand-mother comforted, pulling me into her arms. Meanwhile, Grandfather pulled the closet door shut, just as the house began to crumble. Miraculously, the closet stayed intact, saving our lives.

"What made you run into the closet?" my grandmother asked after we were dug out.

"I heard a voice. It told me to run into the closet," I said, still shaking.

"Thank You, God," I heard Grandfather pray, gratefully.

"Your guardian angel was looking out for you," Grandma said, stroking my face. "And he will continue to do so, don't you ever forget that."

Grandmother's words comforted me, and the fear grip-ping my heart subsided.

After surveying the bomb-ravaged city, Grandfather de-cided we would be safer in a rural area. But we didn't stay safer for long. When spring 1945 arrived, so did the Soviet troops, and we lived under Soviet occupation for almost two years.

In the fall of 1947, a Russian soldier helped us escape to Austria. There, we joined throngs of other refugees in Displaced Persons Camps. That is what we had become—displaced peo-ple without a country. Fortunately, a brighter future lay ahead because people of a distant land named America opened their hearts and country to us. Their courage and compassion, coupled with an ever-present Creator who continually proves His love for us, gave us hope and a new life.

MINE FIELD MIRACLE

by Lt. Col. Robert B. Robeson,
U.S. Army (Ret.), Lincoln, Nebraska

nfantry platoon walked into a mine field. Seven urgent
U.S.- WIA [wounded in action]."

When I read the assignment, trepidation filled me. I
was stationed for a week at Hawk Hill, an infantry and
artillery base south of Da Nang, South Vietnam, as a "dustoff" pilot and operations officer. "Dustoff" was the radio call
sign used by crews who flew unarmed helicopters into shooting situations to evacuate the wounded or dead.

Even though I'd flown many missions under fire, the
mission sheet could still create trepidation. Especially if it
indicated "insecure landing zone," "ground troops surrounded
and under fire" or anything involving "mine field."

As we hurried to our bird, I knew I'd rather go a few
rounds with George Foreman than land in this zone. But
seven Americans wouldn't make it without us. It was our job
and we had to go. We could do nothing else. . .but pray.

En route to the site, I contacted the ground unit radio-
telephone operator, who said, "I have people lying all over the
place. We walked into booby traps and anti-personnel mines."

"We're three minutes out. Are you sure the area for landing is clear?" I asked.

He paused. "Uh, yeah, Dusty. It's all clear."

In eight hundred combat missions, I'd learned some
people mistakenly believed we wouldn't land if they were
taking fire, surrounded, or facing other unsavory things. So
they sometimes didn't mention these things. "Just remember

if I sit down on a mine, it will be a long time before another bird can get out here. I'd appreciate it if you'd recheck the landing area," I said.

I prayed, as I always did before a tactical approach, for our protection and that of our patients. I knew God promised to protect those who called upon Him. Then I approached the spot they'd marked with a red smoke grenade, and planted our skids on either side of the billowing smoke. We quickly loaded the seven mangled bodies. I "pulled pitch" and headed back to our battalion aid station.

I forgot about this mission after it was over. But about a week later, an infantry first lieutenant and his enlisted driver walked in, asking, "Sir, does Dustoff Six-Zero-Five fly out of here?"

"That's me," I replied.

He was a couple of inches shorter than my six-foot height, with vivid blue eyes and light hair. He introduced himself as the platoon leader who'd led his men into the mine field the previous week. After thanking us, he weaved a narrative that increased my pulse.

"The grass was tall where you landed," he began, "so it was hard to visually check. After you left, we discovered the triple prongs of a Bouncing Betty mine sticking out of the ground."

He hesitated. "It only takes eight pounds of pressure to set it off, yet your left skid landed on top of it and mashed it. We laid out some C4 [plastic explosive]. When it blew, the whole top of the hill came off. The anti-tank mine buried beneath that Bouncing Betty was at least two hundred pounds."

Goose bumps covered my body. The Bouncing Betty was an American mine that the Viet Cong had captured and used against us. Unknowingly, I'd landed on top of both mines. . .with neither detonating.

After years of thinking about this, I've realized it's impossible for a person to value something he doesn't know about. If that lieutenant hadn't shown up, I'd never have known what God saved me from. On further reflection, several questions make me shake my head:

1. How did he remember my call sign after that length of time?
2. Why would an infantry lieutenant who was responsible for leading his men into a mine field where seven were seriously wounded drive forty miles over a dangerous dirt road to tell me this?
3. How did he know where to find me, and how did he have time to do so?
4. After traveling for hours in an open jeep in stifling tropical heat, why weren't the man's jungle fatigues sweat-stained like everyone else's? Why did he look as if he'd just had a shower?
5. And why did he drive past our detachment orderly room—the first place a military visitor goes to announce his presence and ask for information in an unfamiliar unit? He came directly to operations. . . where I just happened to be on that day.

I can't "prove" anything. But I know that God has always been beside me, fully in control. I have no doubt I experienced the companionship of an unseen world on both that mission and in the mysterious encounter. This led me to a higher level of faith and provided the courage and strength I needed to complete my combat tour as commander of that unit.

Do I believe in angels? Without a doubt. Do I believe

those two "strangers" had a heavenly heritage? Perhaps I did entertain angels unaware that day. I remember the strength and kindness reflected in those intense blue eyes. An aura of warmth surrounded this encounter, like being brushed by angels' wings. More than thirty years later, I haven't forgotten these two incredible events. Maybe that is why Pope Paul VI allegedly said, "Look up to heaven when you fly, and fear nothing."

Previously printed in *Signs of the Times,* March 2002.

KACEY'S TRUST

by Kristine Vick,
Columbia, South Carolina

Remember the vivid pictures capturing Columbine student Patrick Ireland as he tumbled from the second-story library window into the arms of SWAT team members below? Just a few feet from that window, another student crouched under a library desk, bleeding from gunshot wounds.

Kacey Ruegsegger was in the library that day when gunmen Dylan Klebold and Eric Harris opened fire. She had been studying when she heard pops in the hall. She didn't think much of them until a teacher yelled, "Get down!" Immediately, Kacey dropped under a computer table, pulled in the chair to shield herself, and began praying.

In an interview a few weeks after the shooting, the blond-haired, blue-eyed girl told me she felt like God was preparing her for the worst.

"I knew I was going to get shot," she said. "I just didn't know how badly. I was expecting the worst; I was expecting to die. I also knew that if I was, I was going to go to heaven." Kacey added, "So, that took some of my fear away. If I was going to die, I knew it would be okay."

A few minutes later, Kacey was shot as one of the gunmen went from desk to desk looking for his next victim. One of the bullets pierced Kacey's shoulder, hand, and neck. She fell forward and groaned.

"When he heard me do that he said, 'Quit your b—in.' I thought for sure I would be shot again, so I rolled over and pretended to be dead," she said.

During those next endless moments, Kacey felt evil in the room. Yet, she also felt God or one of His angels with her under the computer table. She realized the full meaning of Jesus' promise in Matthew 28:20: "And surely I am with you always, to the very end of the age."

Through strong faith and determination, Kacey worked to rehabilitate her shoulder. Now God is helping her make a U-Turn to rehabilitate her emotions. She trusts that He will not let her down.

DEVASTATION AT DAWN

by Gloria Cassity Stargel, Gainesville, Georgia,
as told by Brenda Harvey

6:20 A.M.: *Buzzzzz!* Our bedside clock jarred me half-awake. I hit the snooze control. Ah! Thirty more minutes. I detected a faint roll of thunder. Last night's weather forecast for Gainesville, Georgia, had issued no severe storm warnings, so I drifted back to sleep. Beside me, my husband, Danny, never stirred.

Five months earlier we had moved into our new home. For the first time, our sons, Chase, ten, and Tyler, twelve, had their own rooms and felt quite grown up. Curled under the blankets on March 20, 1998, I was oblivious to what was happening outside.

6:34 A.M.: "Mom! Dad!" Chase stood in our bedroom door. "I think you need to wake up."

I propped up on one elbow. My son was shaken. "What's wrong, Chase? You're never up this early."

"Something's not right, Mom. The lights just went out."

Something's not right, I realized with a start. The air feels strange. Just then I heard it. A monster thunder boom that wasn't letting up. It was getting closer. There was no doubt. *TORNADO!*

"Danny! Danny!" I shook my husband. "Wake up. Hurry!"

"Get to the basement, quick!" Danny shouted as he yanked on a pair of pants. I grabbed a robe and raced behind Chase toward the basement stairs. Passing through the kitchen, I saw the walls and doors bulged outward. Through the windows, a gray mass swirled wildly, a mass so thick I couldn't see the porch railings.

At the same moment, our fire alarm shrilled its warning. The outside tornado horn blasted, trying to compete with the twister's roar. Then an eerie silence settled over everything. Except for the intermittent signal from our smoke alarm, all was deathly quiet. Dear God in heaven, help us!

"Go on down, Chase!" I instructed him. I flew into Tyler's room. His bed was empty. At the top of the stairs, I yelled, "Tyler, are you down there?" I heard a frightened "Yes."

"Both of you?"

"Yes."

"Hurry, Danny, hurry!" I hollered. We were about to take a direct hit. "Danny!" A vacuum, created by the tornado, swallowed my screams.

The house began to strain and moan. Starting down the steps, I hesitated. *Where is Danny? What should I do? I need to be with the children. But I can't leave him up here!*

Seconds later, the choice was made for me.

6:35 A.M.: Unleashed fury struck full force at two hundred miles an hour—an F4 tornado. Terrified, I gripped the handrail as I again shouted for Danny. Suddenly the house exploded. Glass shattered. Wood splintered. Shingles ripped off the roof and rafter beams fell. The stone fireplace crashed. Unidentified objects became missiles. Sheet rock dust from pulverized walls and ceilings filled the air. The shrieking wind was deafening.

A wall beside me tore away. I was pulled one way, then another. Shards of glass and bits of concrete block bombarded me. Out of the corner of my eye I spotted a huge black thing flying through the air just before it hit my head. The force sent me careening down the stairs. Everything went black for a few seconds. Yet my subconscious kept saying, *The children.*

You've got to stay alert for the children.

The roar was silenced. I forced my eyes open. Chase and Tyler stood there, soaking wet. All the water had been sucked out of the downstairs commode and the boys were drenched.

"Are you both okay?"

"Yes," they answered shakily. "Where is Daddy?"

Danny! Oh, Lord, is he dead? "You boys stay here," I instructed.

The stairs were blocked with debris. I pushed aside boards with protruding nails and lifted part of a door. Finally, I made it to the top. I couldn't believe my eyes. In fifteen seconds our new home had been destroyed. Only one wall remained standing—the back wall of our breakfast/sunroom. Even the three windows were unbroken. Danny's blue and white Ford pickup and our black Jimmy had been blown into the laundry area, totaled.

"Danny?" I called tentatively.

"Brenda?" he responded.

"Danny! Danny, where are you? Are you hurt?" I saw him crawling over the truck and picked my way toward him.

"No, Brenda, don't come this way! Too much glass. And hot wires. Are the boys safe?"

"Yes, downstairs."

"Go back to them and come out the basement door."

A few minutes later, we met in the front yard. Standing there shivering in our bare feet, we were too much in shock to comprehend what we were seeing. Everything we owned was gone. But we had each other and that's what really mattered. Thank You, God. Thank You.

"Where were you, Danny? Why didn't you come on right behind us?"

He was almost too embarrassed to explain. "I stopped to

muffle the smoke alarm. I was afraid it would disturb the neighbors."

"Danny, you could have gotten us both killed!"

"Don't I know it! I guess I was still half asleep and not thinking clearly. But when the back door flew off beside me, I knew I had waited too long. I just fell down, right where I was. A piece of sheet rock fell on top of me, protecting me. And now that I see where my truck ended up, I know it protected me as well."

It was true. Danny's truck served as a barrier on his left side; the only standing wall in the sunroom was on his right.

Danny suffered minor cuts and bruises. My scalp was embedded with concrete-block chips and glass shards, and my hair—encrusted with red mud—stuck straight out. My parents' house wasn't in the tornado's path, so my dad drove around fallen power lines to take me to the hospital. X-rays ruled out a concussion or broken toe.

When I returned home, Danny was standing in the ruins holding a crumpled birdcage. "Oh, no. Chipper!" Our bright yellow parakeet's cage had been by the fireplace in the living room. We abandoned hope of ever seeing him again.

Two days later, Danny and Tyler were cleaning up the rubble when they heard a faint chirp. Carefully they moved a pile of fireplace rocks. Buried under one rock lay a cold and frightened Chipper—unharmed.

The boys' beds were never found, but part of ours landed on top of my sister's house a half-mile away. The metal frame remains of our camper, which had been parked on the right side of the house, landed on the left side. We also discovered the large object that had hit me on the head—the drum of our neighbor's dryer.

Days later, Chase and I were alone. I asked, "Honey, what

woke you that morning? Whatever it was saved our lives."

Chase hesitated. "I didn't know how to tell you," he started. "I can't say for sure what woke me the first time, but I got up and looked out the window, then went back to bed. That's when it happened. Something—or someone—moved a hand across the back of my hair. I knew I was supposed to come wake you."

He gave me a look which said, You're not going to believe this. "Mom, it was my guardian angel. I didn't see her but I know it was."

"Oh, yes, Chase, I believe you," as I grabbed him in a bear hug, recalling that within moments of his leaving his room, that room was obliterated along with Tyler's room and ours.

Without warning? It appears that we got an advance warning after all. I know God brought us through that tornado. When future storms rage about me, of whatever kind, I can rely on his care.

Previously printed in *The Christian Reader,* March/April 2002.

GOD
ALLOWS
U-TURNS

PRAYER

Ask and it will be given to you;
seek and you will find;
knock and the door will be opened to you.

MATTHEW 7:7

EMBERS OF LOVE

by Kirsten Oschwald,
Louisville, Colorado

Los Alamos, New Mexico, was a government town—born in 1943 to house scientists intent on creating the world's most advanced, destructive weapon. Their success hastened the end of World War II, in clouds of atomic fire, smoke, and ash that changed the world.

Kathleen's parents were part of Los Alamos from the start. She was born on "the Hill" and into the world of technology soon after the war ended. She grew up in this close-knit community that was proud of its heritage and independence.

Plagued with health problems from childhood, Kathleen didn't marry when others her age paired off. She found purpose in loving and caring for her aging parents. But in 1998, Kathleen's parents died within months of each other. The family's home and her dog were the only physical connection she had to memories of a beautiful family life. Her personal knowledge of God's love sustained her during those sad days.

With the loss of her parents, Kathleen had arrived at the end of one road. It was time to turn in a new direction. She prayed for God's guidance but had one more trial to pass through before her dreams would be fulfilled. . .a trial by fire.

A few miles away, yet worlds apart, another story of faith was unfolding.

Don came to the Southwest a few years after the war ended with his young wife, Virginia, and their three children. The family settled in New Mexico, and eventually eight children graced their home.

Virginia had been raised in her family's faith, but Don never felt connected to spiritual things. Instead, besides his family, he poured himself into architecture. Eventually, the family moved into a house that Don designed just for them. After years of Don's creating beautiful spaces for others, it was wonderful to have a home born of Don's imagination, which came to life on the edge of a lovely, forest-filled canyon.

A decade later, Virginia suffered a stroke, and Don turned his energies to caring for his partner of forty-four years. During this difficult time, he learned of God's love and providence. He prayed sincerely and soon began to realize the gift of grace. God answered Don's pleas for Virginia's life for ten more years that softened and refined Don, giving him a tremendous sense of purpose and growth.

On a snowy night early in 1999, Virginia surrendered to a second stroke. Her children's grief was compounded by worry for their father, as they watched him descend into overwhelming sadness. Don's lonely days and nights were occasionally broken by visits from children and grandchildren. He tried to focus on work, but nothing filled the void of Virginia's absence.

With the loss of his wife, Don had arrived at the end of one road. It was time to turn in a new direction. He prayed for God's guidance. But before his dreams would be fulfilled, he had to pass through one more trial. . .a trial by fire.

The morning of May 4, 2000, dawned cloudless and windy. On this day, the National Park Service ignited a "prescribed burn," a controlled fire to clear small trees and undergrowth. But the winds stirred anarchy within the little fire, and it gathered strength.

Early the next morning, the fire burned out of control,

and it was christened the Cerro Grande (Big Hill) Fire. In the following days, the President declared Cerro Grande a national disaster. Despite heroic efforts by a vast emergency force, the fire continued to grow.

Several days later, Cerro Grande jumped a fire line and invaded Los Alamos Canyon, near Don's home. During the evacuation, Don only had time to get his dog, a few clothes and pictures, and the original house plans. Meanwhile, on the other side of the canyon, Kathleen managed to take her dog, a few clothes and pictures, and some family mementos.

Don took refuge with a son in Santa Fe, and Kathleen moved into a temporary shelter. Each watched the news reports. Their worst fears came true as they learned Cerro Grande had destroyed their homes, along with four hundred others. Los Alamos looked like a war zone—chimneys rising from the ashes of homes, skeletons of burned cars, and charred trees. Miraculously, Cerro Grande claimed no human lives as it devoured more than forty-eight thousand acres.

In the dark days that followed, Kathleen and Don continued to pray and seek God's instruction. Each felt that the heavenly Father would shape this situation for good. Each believed He would lead them through the valley of shadows.

Help poured into Los Alamos. The government created a short-term neighborhood of mobile homes at the far end of town—where Don and Kathleen lived just four homes apart.

After months of emotional healing, life slowly began to look normal in the mobile home village. Don began an effort to beautify the neighborhood.

Kathleen's prayers for guidance began to bear fruit on a sunny autumn afternoon. She first met Don at the community mailbox. He introduced himself by saying he was carving a sign, entitled "The Phoenix," to hang at the neighborhood's entrance. To hang the sign, he needed the residents' signatures on a petition. He invited Kathleen to drop by his home to sign the petition. The next day, she accepted his invitation, and they learned they had many things in common.

They were two souls alone who had suffered great personal losses. Each felt stirrings of hope as they talked. That first meeting led to many more visits and to the rebuilding of their lives.

Kathleen shared her religious convictions with Don, and Don studied and grew. He soon chose Kathleen's creed as his own and was baptized. Don's daily walk with God grew from a quiet, internal conversation to a vibrant, outward expression of devotion to Jesus Christ.

About eighteen months after the fire, Don and Kathleen were married in Kathleen's childhood church. Don's eight children, their spouses and children, and a few of Kathleen's friends and extended family witnessed this beautiful event.

Kathleen, once so alone in the world, had gained her fondest dream—a loving husband and a complete, close, supportive family. Don, once so desolate, had gained a new purpose with a new companion to love and nurture.

Holding to their faith and praying for God's guidance amid darkness, these seekers were rewarded in a way neither had imagined. The trial each endured brought them to a new horizon, together, firm in the conviction of God's care.

After it all, Don and Kathleen rebuilt the house on the canyon's edge. As the final touch, he hung the sign that he had first made for the old neighborhood: The Phoenix.

They were given beauty for ashes.

TASK AT HAND
by Marilyn Phillips,
Bedford, Texas

P resident John F. Kennedy has been shot and is not expected to live," our principal announced.

My junior high school teacher stood as stiff as a mannequin. Tears streamed down her face as she rushed to her desk for tissues. But they weren't for her. She insisted that each student take one. Normally guys would refuse such a gesture, but not on this day. Everyone took a tissue.

"How can this be?" my friend sobbed.

Our teacher continued down the rows, kneeling and whispering to each student, "Pray for our country."

Sobbing echoed through the hallways as students and faculty tried to grasp the reality of what had happened. Questions raced through my impressionable mind. Could someone really have shot our president? Who would do such an atrocious thing? Would our beloved President Kennedy live or die?

Our teacher returned to her desk and pulled out a scheduled test. We were in shock. How could she think about tests and grades? Quietly, she placed an exam on each desk.

"Students, we just heard devastating news, and we don't know what the outcome will be," the teacher noted. "Focus on the task at hand. We must complete this test. So, do your best."

As we completed the test and left the classroom, everyone received a hug and another tissue from the teacher. Later that day, I heard the devastating news that President Kennedy had died.

My world didn't seem safe anymore, and I felt confused. The assassination scene was replayed constantly on television. It was like a nightmare. I was awake all night in tears, but my teacher's words rang in my heart.

When we returned to school the next day, I dreaded the test results. Grades were so important to me and I was sure this one would be poor. But when our teacher passed out the papers, she said all of the grades were higher than usual. I was relieved to see an A on my test. Now I understand that our teacher was right to give the test, and she gave us advice right out of the Bible. She had encouraged us to continue to work in times of distress because strength would flow to us. Scripture describes it another way in Proverbs 24:10 (NAS): "If you are slack in the day of distress, your strength is limited."

Years have passed and many devastating American Moment events have affected our lives. I can't remember where I was during every historic event, but the words and actions of my teacher in 1963 have touched my heart forever. She ministered to each student with her kindness and courage.

1 Thessalonians 5:11 says, "Therefore encourage one another and build each other up, just as in fact you are doing."

Right before our eyes, our teacher became a living illustration of the message. She touched our young, impressionable hearts when she asked us to pray for our nation. We were reminded 1 Thessalonians 5:17 (KJV), "Pray without ceasing."

My teacher's advice that devastating day in 1963 continues to guide me decades later. "Focus on the task at hand, minister to others, and always pray for our great nation."

IN THE MIDST OF TEARS

by Miriam Añeses,
Ridgewood, New York

As I climbed out of bed, a tenderness in my ankle and foot reminded me of the fall I'd had a few weeks earlier. After I had my devotions and got dressed for work, I decided an express bus ride to work, instead of the subway trip, would be easier on my feet. At least I could get a seat on the bus and avoid the stairs I'd face on the subway.

Sitting on the bus, I noted that the Manhattan skyline looked spectacular. Beautiful silvery buildings reached up to heaven against a gorgeous blue background. Traffic on the Long Island Expressway was heavy but moving, and I arrived at my office just a few minutes before 9 A.M.

"The World Trade towers are on fire," our receptionist exclaimed as I got off the elevator. A group had already gathered in the conference room, where we had an unobstructed view of the towers. We watched silently as flames turned to black, billowy smoke.

"How can this happen?" someone asked. "How can anyone accidentally hit the towers? You can't miss them."

"The plane must have been in trouble and lost control," someone else theorized. I hoped it was only an accident. My worst fears were confirmed when, fifteen minutes later, a second plane slammed into Tower Two. We realized this was no accident.

The next few hours were bone-chilling. Was this war? What about the people on those planes, the office workers, and the people on the streets? Hundreds must be dead and hurt, I speculated. I shuddered as I wondered about their final thoughts. Then I wondered if anyone I knew was involved.

Next, the two towers collapsed within half an hour of each other. I went from paralyzing shock to tears in seconds. Whoever was still in those buildings didn't have a chance. I covered my face and sobbed. I kept my eyes closed, as if that could block out what I had seen.

Psalm 46:1–2 came to mind: "God is our refuge and strength, an ever-present help in trouble. Therefore we will not fear, though the earth give way and the mountains fall into the heart of the sea." Just then, my friend Bridget grabbed my hand.

"Let's go pray," she said. We went to my office and closed the door. I reached for my Bible and read from Psalm 46 before we prayed. I felt God's overwhelming, all-encompassing peace that is beyond our understanding. It was as if God was wrapping protective arms around me.

In the next few hours, the city shut down. People scrambled to get home however they could. Thousands walked over many of the bridges connecting Manhattan with the rest of the city. Ferry service was available for commuters from New Jersey and Connecticut. Some of us waited it out. No one could work. Instead, we tried to reach family and friends. Telephone service was erratic, but E-mail still worked. That was how I let my family know I was safe.

I did not lose a loved one that morning. Whatever I felt could not compare with the grief engulfing those who had lost loved ones. The poignancy of people walking the streets with photographs of their missing friends and relatives, clinging to any trace of hope they could muster, was eye-opening. In the midst of tears I made a U-Turn as I began to see life with a new perspective.

A few days later, I read Jesus' prayer for His followers (John 17). He did not ask for His disciples to be spared from problems. Instead, He asked God to keep them from evil. It struck me that Jesus may not necessarily have been referring to evil strictly from external sources. He may also have been referring to evil that pollutes our minds and spirits with fear, hatred, anger, doubt, and hopelessness. From His prayer, we learn that only the Spirit of God can protect and renew our spirits and keep us from being overwhelmed by evil.

We have a triumphant God. Evil has raised its fist at God and His people since the beginning of time, but Satan's reach is limited. Although we may feel defeated, God is our strength and in Him we have victory.

I did not make any New Year's resolutions on January 1, 2002, but I did have a September 11 transformation. I am thankful for God's patience with me. When I spend time with Him, even when I deal with weakness, failure, anger, or depression, God reminds me that He is always in control. Nothing gets by Him—not a single tear. I thank Him for the comfort and strength only He can give.

PLUM PURPLE PRAYERS

by Janet Lynn Mitchell,
Orange, California

"M om, I've found exactly what I want for Christmas! It will look great in my room!"

Jenna's dream gift was a thirteen-foot wallpaper mural of Manhattan's skyline. I didn't share Jenna's taste in interior design. We'd spent hours together, shopping and contemplating ways in which she could redecorate her room. I'd shown her flowers in pinks and yellows, and she had escorted me back to take "one more look" at lower Manhattan at dusk, fashioned in plum purple and blues.

"It's cool, Mom. I love it! Can't you see? The city is alive, and its lights reflect a silhouette of New York off the water. Look—there are even two American flags flying proudly!"

I saw them, two American flags, the size of small safety pins high atop the World Trade Center towers. To me, the mural reflected a busy city, full of action and little peace. Nevertheless, this was for Jenna's room. I realized any flowers Jenna may ever display would be in a vase, then purchased the Manhattan Skyline wallpaper.

In just weeks, my sixteen-year-old's bedroom took on a new look. The nightlights of the Manhattan Bridge, Empire State Building, and Twin Towers stretched across her walls. Curtains, a bedspread, and a lamp converted Jenna's California hideaway into the glittering lights of New York City.

Each night since she was born, I've eased my way into my daughter's room at night. I've asked Jenna about her day and listened to her dreams. Often we've studied the skyline, pointing out places we someday want to visit. We pointed to different buildings, pondering what their occupants might have done that day. Night after night I'd point to the towers, sometimes even laying my hand across them saying, "Let's pray for the people who work here."

Jenna responded, "Mom, I pray for them every night."

That wallpaper has now graced Jenna's room for more than a year. Life in New York City has drastically changed because of September 11, 2001. So has our view of the skyline. But Jenna's room remains unchanged. The Twin Towers still stand tall, adhered to Jenna's walls. Those two little flags the size of safety pins remain—untouched—declaring our freedom.

I now see what wasn't clear a year ago. It's more than okay for moms and daughters to differ in their likes. For God gave Jenna her taste in interior design and her desire for a wall mural of Manhattan. For an entire year, Jenna had prayed for people she didn't know, and for a city she had never seen. How grateful I am that I gave Jenna the freedom to follow her heart.

I still find my way to Jenna's room each night. We talk about her day and her plans for tomorrow. Yet, just before I kiss her good night a lump forms in my throat. I try to speak as I point toward Jenna's wall mural.

"I know, Mom," she whispers while gazing at her walls. "I'm still praying."

ESCAPE FROM TOWER TWO

by Robert Fox,
Holmes, New York

I had arrived at the office about fifteen minutes early and was quickly scanning my E-mail. Then the lights blinked for a fraction of a second, and I heard a low rumble. I assumed a maintenance cart was being pushed nearby, or that an automated window washer was descending the 110 stories of World Trade Center Tower Two. What really caught my attention, though, was a fluttering noise from outside.

I walked to the windows that overlook the World Trade courtyard. The scene reminded me of a tickertape parade, only the tickertape was eight-and-a-half-by-eleven-inch printed pages, file folders, and wafting sheets of metal.

I felt lost in this scene for what seemed like an eternity, before someone strongly suggested we leave the building. I grabbed my briefcase and urged coworkers sitting around me to leave too. We had often commented that our twenty-sixth floor offices were a godsend. It was one of the shortest elevator rides in either tower. We did not fully appreciate the gift from God until that day.

No alarms were ringing. No one was screaming in fear. Simple concern led us to the fire escape. During the long walk down, we speculated, assuming a window had blown out on a higher floor and the effect of wind and pressure was causing the paper parade. We found no smoke or unusual smell in the fire escape. Nothing to be concerned about.

The scene at the bottom of the fire stairs was more spectacular. Looking into the courtyard from the atrium, we saw the shower of paper had grown and now included glass, metal, and insulation. We took the escalator down another flight to the mall level. People still remained calm, although now noticeably concerned.

When we reached the street, I saw the damage to Tower One, as well as flames, debris, and smoke. Someone suggested we keep heading east. We didn't discuss. We just moved.

As we crossed the street, the airplane heading for Tower Two made contact. I felt the impact, the heat, and the shock of the hit. Everyone around me screamed in fear. I struggled to help those who had fallen in front of me so they wouldn't be trampled. I was scared.

Debris rained on us as we hurried further east. The sky grew grayer, and the air grew heavier. I turned around to see that both towers were ablaze. People had speculated about a plane crash when we left the building. The idea of two crashes was simply unfathomable.

Just ahead, small factions of my team had managed to group together. We decided to stay together and head north. We stopped every few blocks to view the Trade Center. The smoke grew thicker, the flames grew more pronounced, and news from street radios filled us in on theories behind the catastrophe.

Cell service was minimal. People stood in long lines at the few working pay phones, anxious to call loved ones. Emergency services shut down streets and redirected traffic away from downtown. Someone received a cell call from a coworker who was alone and near Union Square. We headed a block west to meet him, where we could see the smoke around the towers. We watched in horror as Tower One collapsed, not knowing that Tower Two had already tumbled.

We continued north twenty blocks to a coworker's

apartment. We flipped between CNN and the local stations to piece together the entire story. We had better luck with the telephone line at the apartment and could speak with or leave messages for our loved ones and coworkers in different buildings. We relayed our location to several other team members and invited them to join us. Someone suggested that we become a command center for the team.

With coordination of the Boston and Hackensack, New Jersey, offices, we assembled a list of everyone we assumed was in the building and started trying to reach these people on cell phones or at their homes. The process continued for hours. Meanwhile, we watched the news and monitored mass transit availability out of the city.

Seeing the news reports show the second plane crash and the collapse of the towers from a Manhattan apartment was as surreal as watching the two towers burn directly. The conversation soon turned to "What-if?" What if we had been on a higher floor? What if our tower had been struck first? What if we had stayed in the building to watch the rain of papers? What if the exodus down the fire stairs had been disorderly? The what-ifs led us to a ghastly conclusion.

I am writing this at about 5 P.M. on September 11, 2001. I am sitting on a train, heading home after one of the most horrifying days of my life. I'm sure I will have to go through this story countless times tonight and recant it many more times in the future. As it is, my cell phone has been ringing nonstop for ten minutes. I guess I am back in an area with working service. At last count, I had nine voice mails to answer.

I will not want to live through this again. I will not want to wake up in a sweat from dreams about this. I don't want to start thinking about details to fill in to this account. I don't want to watch the news again, to hear body counts, to deal with a pending relocation of my office space. I don't want to let the emotions catch up to me and leave me a sobbing mess in the corner of a darkened room, but I know that I will have no choice. These actions, as the plane crashes, will be out of my control.

I will pray for those who did not survive the incidents of September 11, 2001. . .and for those who did. I will pray as I have never prayed before.

TWILIGHT PRAYER

by Susan Farr Fahncke,
as told by Daniel Fahncke, Fort Pierce, Florida

I stared at the photo in my hands, faded with time and dark at the edges. Twilight was falling when the picture was taken. The memories of Vietnam flooded back. Vietnam was my first exposure to death, and we lived closely with it on a daily basis. I was an eighteen-year-old kid who would have rather been home in the States dragging the boulevard than giving thirteen months of my life to watching, living, being a part of a horror that those who weren't there can never fully understand.

Prayer was a constant, my most frequent plea, "God, please get me out of here alive," followed by "Why?" "Why him, why not me?" when buddies died. It seemed so senseless. Yet still I prayed, almost ceaselessly, during my entire time on Vietnam soil. Prayer kept me sane.

The photo in my hand trembled slightly as the memories washed over me. We rarely enjoyed laughter or relaxation. Every waking and sleeping moment we were on our guard, always prepared to kill or be killed. When the photo was taken, my detail had been holed up in a North Vietnamese-infested area, in the middle of heavy danger. We fought weary battles for days on end; one fading into another.

This day was a reprieve from the war. A day when it had all gotten to be too much and we needed an outlet. That day we played hooky from war. We went swimming. Like children, we laughed and splashed and allowed ourselves a day off from Vietnam. I remember the bliss, the knots in my stomach easing for a few hours as I let myself just be eighteen for awhile.

The day was blessed with God's grace as we really lived—not merely survived. Our laughter still echoes in my memory—the river calm and almost peaceful, sparkling as the sun shone upon it, our day in the sun the best therapy, aside from going home, those young soldiers needed.

We sunbathed, and for a few precious hours, we were just kids, letting loose. Gunfire never erupted, death never stole that moment from us, and God watched over and gave us that day. Having had a few good hours of much-needed relaxation, I was thankful for the Lord's protection amid the shadow of death. That single day provided a U-Turn with God in many ways, turning me closer to Him as my faith was strengthened—renewed.

The Twenty-third Psalm ran through my mind as the sun lowered and I knelt along the riverbank to thank God for our safe haven. My buddy snapped the picture that now rests in my hands and tells the rest of the story.

It is twilight in Vietnam. It is the middle of a war. In the middle of enemy territory, we survived a blissful day under God's watchful eye, and I am on the riverbank, on my knees, in grateful prayer. My twilight prayer in Vietnam.

"The Lord is my shepherd; I shall not want. He maketh me to lie down in green pastures: he leadeth me beside the still waters. He restoreth my soul: he leadeth me in the paths of righteousness for his name's sake. Yea, though I walk through the valley of the shadow of death, I will fear no evil: for thou art with me; thy rod and thy staff they comfort me. Thou preparest a table before me in the presence of mine enemies: thou anointest my head with oil; my cup runneth over. Surely goodness and mercy shall follow me all the days of my life: and I will dwell in the house of the Lord forever."

PSALM 23 KJV

ACKNOWLEDGMENTS

The phrase "God Allows U-Turns" truly does sum up my life. As a former "prodigal daughter," I can now see clearly how many times my heavenly Father was there to rescue me, guide me, and give me the wisdom to turn around in my tracks and retreat from ways destined to bring me to destruction. Today, I cannot imagine my life without God's love, without the knowledge that Jesus Christ died for me. I am a living, breathing example of how a life can be drastically changed. . .with God's help. I really am what the press has come to call: "The U-Turns Poster Girl."

The book you hold in your hands today is the fourth volume in a series of short-story collections that we know are encouraging and uplifting tens of thousands of people around the world.

And for that I graciously thank. . .

The thousands of author/contributors whose stories made us laugh, cry, and praise the Lord with joyful alleluias: You are gems beyond value. May God continue to shine His light on your lives.

My dearest husband, Kevin: Christ is my foundation, and you are the cornerstone of my life. Without you, success would not taste as sweet.

My son, Christopher: Outstretched arms are waiting for you. . .those of Jesus Christ and mine. It is never too late to make a U-Turn. I miss you. I love you.

The special people in my life who show me often how God's love is all around us: Dolores Gappa, Cheryll Hutchings, Mandy Bottke, Kermit Bottke, Kyle Bottke, Lisa Copen, Debbye Butler, Linda Lagnada, Pastor Ron Wik, and Sharol Wik. A special thank-you to Chip MacGregor, my publishing team at Barbour/Promise Press, the U-Turns Grassroots Promotional and Volunteer Groups, Linda Evans Shepherd and the AWSA group of awesome ladies, Fred Littauer and Florence Littauer and my UpperCLASS ladies, Marita Littauer and all the amazing CLASS Instructors, Jennifer Johnson, Ramona Richards, and the hundreds of U-Turns contributors whose E-mails keep me encouraged and blessed on a daily basis.

Above all, I give praise and thanks to my Holy Father. His unconditional love and the plan He had for me even before I was born helped me leave behind the ways of the world, ways that were leading me down paths of destruction, hitting one dead end after another. The Lord alone turned me around and set my path straight. Thank You, my most holy Lord, for giving me the wisdom to understand not only that God Allows U-Turns, but that no matter what I have done I can continue to turn my heart and mind toward You. You will always forgive me; You will always love me; You will always bring me the peace I need. Because it is so very true. . .God Allows U-Turns!

ALLISON

WE CAN ALL
CELEBRATE THE GIFT!

Dear reader, I can't leave without asking one most important question. Do you have a personal relationship with the eternal God? I'm not talking about "getting a religion." I'm talking about "getting a relationship." You may have read every word of this book and yet never experienced the peace and strength and hope that our authors have shared with you here.

I spent decades of my life looking for fulfillment in all the wrong places. Today, I have peace, strength, and hope because there was a time in my life when I accepted Jesus as my personal Savior. That is what I mean by getting a "relationship," not a "religion."

The way is simple: It takes only three steps.
- Admit that you are a sinner: "For all have sinned and fall short of the glory of God" Romans 3:23.
- Believe that Jesus is God the Son and He paid the wages of your sin: "For the wages of sin is death [eternal separation from God], but the gift of God is eternal life in Christ Jesus our Lord" Romans 6:23.
- Call upon God: "If you confess with your mouth, 'Jesus is Lord,' and believe in your heart that God raised him from the dead, you will be saved" Romans 10:9.

Our Web site has a "Statement of Faith" page that you might find interesting and comforting. On that page you will find helpful (and hopeful) links to other spiritually uplifting Web pages. Please visit us at http://www.godallowsuturns.com.

Salvation is a very personal thing. It is between you and God. I cannot have faith enough for you; no one can. The decision is yours alone. Please know that this wonderful gift of hope and healing is available to you. You can celebrate the Gift! You need only reach out and ask for it. It is never too late to make a U-Turn toward God. . .no matter where you have been or what you have done. Please know that I am praying for you.

God's peace and protection always,
ALLISON GAPPA BOTTKE

Future Volumes of
GOD ALLOWS U-TURNS

The stories you have read in this volume were submitted by readers just like you. From the very start of this inspiring book series, it has been our goal to encourage people from around the world to submit their slice-of-life, true short stories for publication.

God Allows U-Turns stories must touch the emotions and stir the heart. We are asking for well-written, personal, inspirational pieces showing how faith in God can inspire, encourage, heal, and give hope. We are looking for human-interest stories with a spiritual application, affirming ways in which Christian faith is expressed in everyday life.

Because of the huge response to our call for submissions, we plan to publish additional volumes in the U-Turns series every year.

Your true story can be from 300–1,500 words and must be told with drama, description, and dialogue. Our writer's guidelines are featured on our Web site, and we encourage you to read them carefully. Or send us an SASE for a copy of the guidelines. Please note the two addresses below.

To Request Guidelines:
GOD ALLOWS U-TURNS
P.O. Box 668 - DEPT. V3
Brunswick, OH 44212

Editorial Offices:
GOD ALLOWS U-TURNS
P.O. Box 717
Faribault, MN 55021-0717

E-mail: editor@godallowsuturns.com
http://www.godallowsuturns.com

Fees are paid for stories we publish, and we will be sure to credit you for your submission. Remember, our Web site is filled with up-to-date information about the book project. Additionally, you might want to take advantage of signing up to be on our free "Hotline Update" list for Internet users. For a list of current *God Allows U-Turns* books open to submissions, as well as related opportunities, visit us at:

http://www.godallowsuturns.com

SHARING THE SUCCESS:
THE GOD ALLOWS U-TURNS
FOUNDATION

One of the most profound lessons in the Bible is that of giving. The Holy Bible is quite clear in teaching us how we are to live our lives. Scripture refers to this often, and never has the need to share with others been so great.

"Give, and it will be given to you. A good measure, pressed down, shaken together and running over, will be poured into your lap. For with the measure you use, it will be measured to you" (Luke 6:38).

In keeping with the lessons taught us by the Lord our God, we are pleased to have the opportunity to donate a portion of the net profits of every *God Allows U-Turns* book to one or more nonprofit Christian charities. These donations are made through the GOD ALLOWS U-TURNS FOUNDATION, a funding mechanism established by Allison Gappa Bottke as a way to share the success of this growing U-Turns outreach ministry.

For details on the beneficiaries of the volume you are now holding, please visit our Web site at: http://www.godallowsuturns.com.

ABOUT OUR EDITORS

ALLISON GAPPA BOTTKE lives in southern Minnesota on a twenty-five-acre hobby farm with her entrepreneur husband, Kevin. She is a relatively "new" Christian, coming to the fold in 1989 as a result of a dramatic life "U-Turn." The driving force behind the God Allows U-Turns Project, she has a growing passion to share with others the healing and hope offered by the Lord Jesus Christ. Allison has a wonderful ability to inspire and encourage audiences with her down-to-earth speaking style as she relates her personal testimony of how God orchestrated a dramatic U-Turn in her life. Lovingly dubbed "The U-Turns Poster Girl," you can find out more about Allison by visiting her information pages on the book's Web site:

    http://www.godallowsuturns.com/aboutauthor.htm

    http://www.godallowsuturns.com/modeling.htm

    http://www.godallowsuturns.com/gappabottke_speakerinfo.htm

CHERYLL MARIE HUTCHINGS was born in Ohio, where she has lived all her life. She and her family live in a rambling ranch home minutes from "civilization," yet secluded enough to enjoy the area wildlife that ambles through her own backyard in abundance. Cheryll and her husband, Robert, are raising two teenage sons, Aaron and Scott. In addition to her work as coeditor of the U-Turns project, Cheryll currently works for the Brunswick Community Recreation Center.

CONTRIBUTING AUTHOR BIOS

BONNIE M. ALBA writes articles on American cultural issues from a biblical perspective. She also teaches Sunday school and Bible studies and is a speaker. She lives with her husband, Vince, a retired army sergeant major who is now a science teacher, in Hanford, California.

MARY EMMA ALLEN writes for children and adults. Her work appears in inspirational and family publications. Her book, *When We Become the Parent to Our Parents,* encourages those with family members suffering from Alzheimer's. Web site: http://homepage. fcgnetworks.net/jetent/mea. E-mail: me.allen@juno.com.

MICHAEL L. ANDERSON lives in Ball Ground, Georgia, with his wife, Kathy. Together they operate a wild bird specialty store. Michael has written newspaper articles and video and music reviews for the *CBA Marketplace* and *Bookstore Journal.* He is an officer in a Christian writers' group.

MIRIAM AÑESES, a native New Yorker, administers an education fellowship program at a major New York City foundation. Her freelance writing includes contributions to *God's Word for Today* (Gospel Publishing) and the book *A Growing Heart,* edited by Kathy Collard Miller (Starburst Publishers, 2001).

SANDY AUSTIN is a school counselor in Lakewood, Colorado. She has a master's degree in counseling, and has worked in education for eighteen years. Sandy has written two books, *Angry Teens and Parents Who Love Them* and *Focus on Your Future.* Sandy's Web site is at http://home.att.net/~sandy-austin.

TAMMERA AYERS resides in St. Marys, Ohio, with her husband and three children. She substitute teaches for the local schools and is active in the children's ministries at her church. Her hobbies include reading, writing, sewing, bike riding, and camping.

NORKA BLACKMAN-RICHARDS lives in New York with her minister husband. She teaches writing and ESL and writes a weekly devotional entitled "From the Heart" at www.coronasda.org. A pastor's child, Norka grew up in Latin America, Europe, and the Caribbean and values this experience as "priceless."

LANITA BRADLEY BOYD is a Fort Thomas, Kentucky, freelance writer. Her writing genes and experience come from her mother, a poet and essayist, and her maternal grandfather, a Tennessee newspaper columnist and storyteller. She and husband, Steve, have worked with the Central Church of Christ, Cincinnati, for twenty-eight years.

MARY RALPH BRADLEY was born in Sumner County, Tennessee, the fouth of nine children to Luther D. and Hester Martin Ralph. Married the day she turned twenty, she had forty wonderful years with Lawrence Bradley. Both were teachers. Since his death in 1984 she has been working as a legal secretary.

ANGEL BROWN is a freelance writer living in New York. Her writing has appeared in *Queens Parent* magazine, *The Montpelier Bridge* newspaper, and the NAWW Weekly E-magazine. You can visit her at http://www.angel-brown.com.

RENIE SZILAK BURGHARDT was born in Hungary and came to the U.S. in the early fifties. Her credits include stories in *Chocolate for Women, Listening to the Animals* series published by *Guideposts, Whispers from Heaven, Angels on Earth,* and many others. She lives in the country and loves observing nature when she's not spending time with her family.

MELISSA CHAVEZ is a middle-aged woman who desires a childlike faith. Married to Steve and mom to Sean, Sierra, and Alani Rose, she is increasingly thankful for family, friendships, laughter, music, writing, Filipino roots, thriving flower gardens, and God's wondrous love.

ANN COOGLER enjoys life in Salem, South Carolina, with her husband, Bill. She is a mother, grandmother, and former teacher. She contributes humorous writing to Writer's Ink writing group and a local newspaper. "My story is WTGG—writing to God's glory." E-mail her at abcoog@mindspring.com.

NANCY CRIPE lives in Minneapolis, Minnesota, with her husband, Brian, and children, Jonathan and Elizabeth. She likes to weave stories by drawing on her years of teaching science, traveling, and making friends from all over. The best day for her is a day beside the sea.

KAREN HARPER DELOACH is the author of *Thirty-One Years and a Stumble.*

She heads up "KD & Kompany," a drama group. This proud mother of three sons is her husband, Bill's, "right hand" in their business. Reach her at P.O. Box 1474, Statesboro, GA, 30459; (912) 489-8838; or e-mail her at kdeloach@frontiernet.net or http://karendeloach.tripod.com.

MARGO DILL is an elementary school teacher in St. Peters, Missouri. She has previously published a children's story entitled *Secrets in Calliope: A Writer's Workshop Magazine* and is working on a Civil War novel for middle grade children.

SUSAN FARR FAHNCKE is the author of *Angel's Legacy* and runs her own inspirational Web site at www.2theheart.com. She has stories in *U-Turns* volumes 1 and 2 and is excited to be part of the series. E-mail Susan at Editor@2theheart.com.

CHARLES FARRELL is a eucharistic minister at Saint Patrick Roman Catholic Church in Southold, New York. Married for forty-five years, he is the father of two beautiful daughters and grandfather of six God-sent grandchildren. Charles is a retired NYC firefighter (twenty-three years) from a three-generation firefighter family.

ROBERT FOX, when not playing with his two beautiful daughters or dreaming up home remodeling projects with his lovely wife, spends his free time as a systems engineer for a large computer firm. Robert and his family live in New York's Dutchess County, an hour north of Manhattan. He claims to be the worst golfer in the state, and quite possibly the world.

CAY A. GIBSON is a wife/mother/writer living in southwest Louisiana. She has been published in a number of Christian and homeschooling magazines. She enjoys reading, traveling, and camping with her family. She is thankful and proud to be an American.

CHARLES GIBSON, after completing his M.A. in psychology, is pursuing a life-long, "impractical" goal of writing full-time. He lives in Centerville, Minnesota, with his wife, Tricia—who doubles as his editor and is a licensed associate marriage and family therapist. Reach him at gwriterdrew@-netscape.net.

TONY GILBERT is a writer and consultant living in Albany, Georgia. An accomplished marathon runner, he is a former teacher, coach, and sports writer. His first book, *Coincidental Encounters,* includes a collection of personal stories.

MAJOR GLEN A. GRADY is from Denver, Colorado, where he lives with his wife and two sons. With more than sixteen years of army service, he is assigned to the Strategic Leadership Division, Headquarters, Dept. of the army. He has served in a variety of command and staff positions.

GRACE M. GRAZIANO is a graduate of CLASS (Certified Personality Training) and contributing author in *Getting Along with Almost Anybody.* Grace shares her stories and inspiration in writing and speaking throughout Florida.

ELIZABETH GRIFFIN lives with her husband and two children in Washington State. She enjoys freelance writing and encouraging women in their walk with the Lord. She leads a support group for moms with special needs children and teaches a women's Bible study in her church.

PATTY SMITH HALL is a board member of the American Christian Romance Writers and is currently working on her third novel. She lives in Hiram, Georgia, with her husband, Dan, and their daughters, Jennifer and Carly.

DR. DON J. HANSON is now retired after many years as a pastor and evangelist. An author and marriage seminar leader, he helped found Bethel West Seminary (San Diego). Reach him at 3330 S. Lowell St., Santa Ana, CA 92707; (714) 751-7824; bonnieh1@worldnet.att.net.

CARLIN RANDALL HERTZ lives in Waldorf, Maryland, and is married to his high school sweetheart, Jonata Hertz. They have two handsome boys, C.J., four, and Jaylin Isaiah, seven months. He is currently working on a fiction novel and serving as a freelance national sports columnist.

SARA HOUY was a sophomore in Littleton, Colorado, during the April 20, 1999, tragedy. She has traveled across the country, speaking about the event and how God used it. She attends college and helps lead the junior and senior high youth groups at her church.

KATHRYN K. HOWARD lives in Rochester, New York. She is a single mother, technical/freelance writer, student, Web editor, and coordinator of Notes to New York and Washington (http://www.notes2nydc.com). She educates the public about bipolar disorder, a disease with which she has a lifelong relationship. Contact her at khatn@aol.com.

MARIE JONES is a widely published writer with more than thirty inspirational book credits, including *God Bless America: Prayers for Our Country; Bless This Marriage;* and *Simple Wisdom.* She also writes and produces children's videos for Gigglebugfarms.com. She is married with one son, Max.

LAROSE KARR is a church secretary and a contributing writer to *God Allows U-Turns* and enjoys speaking to women. She believes her writing is a gift from God and gives Him all the glory! You can reach her at rosiebay@kci.net.

KATHLEEN COUDLE KING is a mom of four, playwright, and author of *Wannabe,* a novel about growing up female in New Jersey. Read more at www.angelfire.com/nd/wannabe.

Writing is important to MARCIA KNOBLOCK, whether she's working as a PC consultant and technical writer; creating poems, stories, and essays; or developing a Bible study guide. She lives in Georgia with her son, James. E-mail: mknoblock@yahoo.com.

MARY A. LACLAIR is a charter member of the Syracuse, New York, Christian Writers' Group, runs Four Emeralds Christian Literary Services/Agency, is a columnist with Press Media Group in Virginia and has been published nationally and internationally in religious and secular markets.

TRINA LAMBERT writes from Colorado, where she lives with her husband, daughter, son, and dog. Her work has appeared in *TWINS Magazine,* Moms Online, Christian Families Online, and the Denver Post. Read more at http://www.trinalambert.com.

PATRICIA LAYE is a multi-published author with recent stories in several Chicken Soup books and *Woman's World* magazine. She is the author of seven novels for Berkley/Jove, Dell, and Zebra. She travels the world with her husband searching for new settings and stories. She lives in south Georgia, the setting for the novel she is writing now.

CARMEN LEAL is a professional speaker, singer, and the author of four books, including *Portraits of Huntington's,* and WriterSpeaker.com. She can be reached at Carmen@writerspeaker.com or visit her Web site at http://www.writer-speaker.com.

MARY J. DIXON LEBEAU is an employment counselor, freelance writer, and newspaper columnist. She lives in West Deptford, New Jersey, with her husband, Scott, and her four children. Mary can be reached at mlebeau@snip.net.

SUZANNE MARTIN worked in the legal field for thirty years as a litigator, speaker, and teacher. She has two grown sons. Retired and living in Naples, Florida, she spends time writing and volunteering as an ESOL (English for Speakers of Other Languages) teacher.

IRIS E. MAY is published in GreenPrints Magazine and Liz Curtis Higgs' book, *Help, I'm Laughing and I Can't Get Up.* She received an award from the army during Desert Storm for New Wives Training. Married thirty-six years, she's a mother, grandmother, and retired oncology nurse.

SANDRA MCGARRITY lives in Chesapeake, Virginia, with her husband of twenty-nine years. They have two grown daughters. Sandra's writing has appeared in Christian magazines and she is the author of a novel, *Woody,* by American House Publishers.

JANET LYNN MITCHELL is an inspirational speaker and author of articles and stories in compilations. Her experience with medical malpractice/fraud resulted in the signing into law California AB2571. Her story, *Taking a Stand,* has inspired thousands. Janet can be reached at Janetlm@ prodigy.net.

MARILYN MORSCH and husband, Bill, have three children and five grandchildren. She volunteers at her church in women's ministries leading Bible studies and is active in her community. As a retired elementary schoolteacher, she tutors first graders in reading.

JOYCE ANNE MUNN lives in West Siloam Springs, Oklahoma. She is retired after teaching elementary school for thirty-nine years. She serves on the national board of Christian Educators Association, an organization for educators in public schools.

KIRSTEN OSCHWALD is a home-based writer, paralegal, virtual assistant, and business owner living in Colorado. She is the grateful beneficiary of many U-Turn miracles in her own life and in the lives of loved ones. You may contact her at kirsten_erika@ivillage.com.

MICHELLE GUTHRIE PEARSON is a wife, mother, freelance writer, and home-based business owner who lives with her family on their farm in northwestern Illinois. Her work has appeared in previous GAUT volumes. You can reach Michelle at http://www.countrymeadowsoapworks.com or at stoneyknoll@lrnet1.com

MARILYN PHILLIPS of Bedford, Texas, has written three books: *A Cheerleader for Life, God Speaks to Cheerleaders,* and *Cheering for Eternity.* Her articles have been published in *God Allows U-Turns,* Volume I, *Chicken Soup for the Surviving Soul, Guideposts, Parent Life, Home Life,* and *Living with Teenagers.*

RHONDA LANE PHILLIPS and her husband are active Gideons. She marvels at how God plants opportunities to share His Word. She and her family live in the Blue Ridge Mountains of Virginia, where she is never far away from pen and paper, writing for children.

DIANE H. PITTS, a lifelong resident of Alabama, has twenty-five years experience as a nurse and physical therapist. As wife, mother, and educator, she writes about practical faith on the homefront as well as the medical arena.

STEPHANIE PLANK lives in Littleton, Colorado, and is very active in the college group at West Bowles Community Church. Stephanie hopes that her story touches your heart and helps to further the kingdom. You can contact her at littletikes20@yahoo.com.

GARY W. PLOURDE SR. is a fifty-two-year-old former marine Vietnam (disabled) veteran who lost his left leg from a grenade explosion in combat. By the grace of God, he overcame. Today, he writes poetry, non-fiction, fiction, and hopefully, one day, a novel or two.

MICHAEL T. POWERS, whose writing appears in fourteen inspirational books, is a youth director, high school girls' coach, and the author of *Straight from the Heart.* For a sneak peek or to join the thousands of worldwide readers on his daily inspirational E-mail list, visit: http://www.HeartTouchers.com. E-mail: MichaelTPowers@AOL.COM

ROBERT ROBESON resides in Lincoln, Nebraska. He flew 987 combat medical missions in South Vietnam (1969–1970), evacuating 2,533 patients. He retired from the U.S. Navy after twenty years as a lieutenant colonel. A freelance writer, he's been published more than six hundred times in 230 publications worldwide.

MARGARET SAYLAR attended Westmont College and graduated from California State University at Sacramento. She and husband, Daniel, have two grown sons. She has seen eleven magazine articles published, and her letter was accepted for *Life's Best Lessons.* Her E-book, *Take My Hand,* is online.

MAUREEN SCHMIDGALL lives in the Midwest with her husband and children, writing historical fiction and raising funds and awareness for Fragile X Syndrome, the leading cause of genetic mental retardation. Maureen hopes for a cure for this disorder, which affects her son.

GAIL SCHUIT and her husband are members of Africa Inland Mission and served on staff at Rift Valley Academy in Kenya for twenty-three years. They currently manage Missionary Retreat Fellowship, providing housing for missionaries on home assignment. They have two teenage children.

JENNIFER SMITH-MORRIS loves to help women realize the forgiveness and love they have in Christ Jesus, and writes and speaks on this topic. She is currently writing a Bible study that teaches and encourages mothers. She lives in Georgia with her husband and three children.

GLORIA CASSITY STARGEL, an assignment writer for *Guideposts* magazine, is author of *The Healing, One Family's Victorious Struggle with Cancer*—an unforgettable story of faith, hope, and love. This award-winning book will encourage anyone facing change or adversity. Contact: 1-800-888-9529 or http://www.brightmorning.com.

TAMARA SWINSON resides in Tulsa, Oklahoma, with her husband and three children. An active home-school mom and student at Tulsa Community College, she relishes the time she gets to use the writing talent that God gave to her! Check out her first published story in *More God Allows U-Turns* entitled "Angel on Earth!"

GAYLE TEAM-SMITH is an inspirational speaker and writer. She is active in community leadership and enjoys decorating and spending time with family. Drawing from life experiences, she seeks to comfort, challenge, and encourage others. Gayle, her husband, Myles, and their children live in Oklahoma. Contact: gayle.smith@lmscpa.com.

LYNN ROATEN TERRELL has been published and broadcast around the world. She owns a public relations agency and TheWebDirectory.com

Network, which she runs from her historic home in Kansas. Her writing portfolio of award-winning pieces is at LynnTerrell.com. She and Amos, an aerospace engineer, have two children.

LINDA TINKER is the author of *Testament,* a musical drama about the life, death, and resurrection of Jesus, and has also composed many praise and worship songs. She has written a number of inspirational pieces for the Internet and church publications. Contact her at lindatinker.tripod.com.

LYDIA S. URE is a pastor's wife in a Windsor, Ontario, church plant. She was a volunteer in pastoral care at the local hospital for many years, but now devotes her time to her husband, children, grandchildren, and freelance writing.

KRISTINE VICK is a former national news reporter for the Christian Broadcasting Network. Her coverage for CBN news included the Columbine and Oklahoma City tragedies. She is currently taking time off from her career to raise her family.

KATHY WHALING lives in Littleton, Colorado, with her husband and their six daughters. She believes God has used her writing to bring Him glory, and to let others know of His grace and unconditional love. She is a volunteer counselor at Riverside Pregnancy Center and is a Sunday school teacher at her church. You may reach her at kwhaling@pcisys.net.

REV. MICHAEL F. WELMER received his master of divinity degree in 1973 from Concordia Theological Seminary in Springfield, Illinois, and has served in the parish ministry for twenty-nine years. He is currently senior pastor of Epiphany Lutheran Church in Houston, Texas.

KARI WEST is the author of *Dare to Trust, Dare to Hope Again: Living with Losses of the Heart* and coauthor of *When He Leaves.* She lives with her second husband, two dogs, and a goat named Sigmund. Visit her Web site www.gardenglories.com. To contact Kari and/or request the free Divorce-Wise Newsletter, write P.O. Box 11692, Pleasanton, CA 94568 or e-mail kariwest@juno.com.

Also Available from Promise Press

GOD ALLOWS U-TURNS
1-58660-300-0

MORE GOD ALLOWS U-TURNS
1-58660-301-9

Coming Soon. . .

GOD ALLOWS U-TURNS:
A Woman's Journey
1-58660-578-X

Paperback, 5"x8", $9.99

Available Wherever Books Are Sold
Or order from:

Promise Press
P.O. Box 719
Uhrichsville, OH 44683
www.promisepress.com

If you order by mail, add $2.00 to your order for shipping.
Prices are subject to change without notice.